At Issue

Are Conspiracy
Theories Valid?

Other books in the At Issue series:

At Issue

Are Conspiracy Theories Valid?

Stuart A. Kallen, Book Editor

GREENHAVEN PRESS

An imprint of Thomson Gale, a part of The Thomson Corporation

Detroit • New York • San Francisco • San Diego • New Haven, Conn.
Waterville, Maine • London • Munich

Bonnie Szumski, *Publisher*
Helen Cothran, *Managing Editor*

© 2006 Thomson Gale, a part of The Thomson Corporation.

Thomson and Star Logo are trademarks and Gale and Greenhaven Press are registered trademarks used herein under license.

For more information, contact:
Greenhaven Press
27500 Drake Rd.
Farmington Hills, MI 48331-3535
Or you can visit our Internet site at http://www.gale.com

LIBRARY OF CONGRESS CATALOGING-IN-PUBLICATION DATA

Are conspiracy theories valid? / Stuart A. Kallen, book editor.
    p. cm. -- (At issue)
  Includes bibliographical references and index.
  0-7377-3431-0 (lib. bdg. : alk. paper) -- 0-7377-3432-9 (pbk. : alk. paper)
  1. Conspiracies. 2. September 11, 2001, terrorist attacks--Miscellanea.
3. Kennedy, John F. (John Fitzgerald), 1917–1963--Assassination--Miscellanea.
4. AIDS (Disease)--Government Policy--Miscellanea. 5. Unidentified flying
objects--Miscellanea. I. Kallen, Stuart A. 1995– . II. At issue (San Diego, Calif.).
    HV6275.A74 2006
    001.9--dc22
                                                                    2005044722

Printed in the United States of America
10 9 8 7 6 5 4 3 2 1

Contents

Introduction

On November 22, 1963, at 12:30 P.M., President John F. Kennedy was fatally shot in front of hundreds of witnesses in Dallas while riding in a presidential motorcade. Within eighty minutes of the assassination, Lee Harvey Oswald was arrested for allegedly killing Dallas police officer J.D. Tippit. Later that evening he was also charged with killing Kennedy. The nation was shocked by the assassination and many Americans feared that the assassination was part of a greater Cold War attack on the United States. However, in 1964 the Warren Report, written by the government commission established to investigate the assassination, concluded that Oswald had acted alone and had not been part of any foreign or domestic conspiracy to kill the president.

The report did not put to rest public speculation about Kennedy's death. On the contrary, as Kennedy assassination expert John McAdams writes, the day the Warren Report was published, "vigorous conspiracy theories commenced, and the whodunit debate has roiled ever since." Speculation about Kennedy's murder has been greatly publicized over the years in more than two thousand books, dozens of television shows, and numerous films. With the introduction of the World Wide Web in the mid-1990s, conspiracy theorists went online and began holding electronic conversations concerning the Kennedy assassination via Internet discussion groups. These groups brought together like-minded conspiracy enthusiasts who generated new conspiracy theories about many other national and world events. By the end of the 1990s, there were hundreds of Web sites that presented various conspiracy theories concerning UFOs, the origins of AIDS, and the deaths of various public figures, including John Lennon, Martin Luther King Jr., and Diana, Princess of Wales.

Since 2001, the number of users visiting conspiracies Web sites has continued to grow at an extraordinary rate. Some of this growth can be attributed to unprecedented occurrences such as the terrorist attacks of September 11, 2001. As with the Kennedy assassination, millions refuse to believe the official account of the events that transpired that day. One anonymous posting on the Web site AboveTopSecret.com expressed a view common among conspiracy theorists:

> It is APPALLING how ignorant the US public and the mainstream media are about the true facts of what really happened on 9/11. There is so much evidence that debunks the [government's] claims about what happened. It is like the public and the mainstream media think that just because the govt says [something] . . . it must be true. Like the govt has a good track record in telling the truth.

Visitors to AboveTopSecret.com and other conspiracy theory Web sites discuss what they consider the many political conspiracies that riddle the nation.

The role the Internet has played in helping spread these conspiracy theories may be seen in the popularity of the video, "9/11: Pentagon Strike." In 2003 Darren Williams, a British systems analyst, set up a Web site featuring a homemade video presentation that questions the official version of the terrorist attack on the Pentagon in 2001. The video uses eyewitness accounts and photographs taken shortly after the attack as evidence for the theory that a missile or military aircraft—and not a hijacked airplane—slammed into the Pentagon.

Williams did little to publicize his Web site other than notifying others about it in an online discussion group to which he belongs. However, members of this group, set up to discuss politics and the paranormal, told others. Within days, the "9/11: Pentagon Strike" video had been downloaded by millions of people throughout the world. Dozens of others posted the video on their personal Web sites, some of which received over 700,000 hits a day.

While it is unknown how many people actually believe the conclusions put forth in the Williams video, its popularity demonstrates a growing hunger for conspiracy theories on the Internet. Although most sites are harmless, skeptics warn that the widespread broadcast of questionable theories can be dangerous. As Evan Harrington writes in *Skeptical Inquirer* magazine, conspiracy theories may "act in a manner similar to racist stereotyping in which the targeted group [such as a government agency] is seen as deviant and deeply immoral. . . . Conspiracy theories offer individuals well-organized enemies against whom the self is defined." These feelings may breed distrust and even violent reactions against authorities. For most, however, conspiracy theories are simply a way to deal with the tragedies of assassination, war, and terrorism. As Michael Barkun, political scientist and expert on the culture of conspiracies, writes,

> Conspiracy theories are one way to make sense of what happened and regain a sense of control. Of course, they're usually wrong, but they're psychologically reassuring. Because what they say is that everything is connected, nothing happens by accident, and that there is some kind of order in the world, even if it's produced by evil forces. I think psychologically, it's in a way consoling to a lot of people.

Whether they serve to calm or incite believers, there is little doubt that conspiracy theories have become a permanent part of the Internet. In a world that is sharply divided politically, millions will continue to speculate about the motives of those in power. Conspiracy theory Web sites provide one more way for people to satisfy their own curiosity about events over which they have little control.

1

The U.S. Government Perpetrated the September 11 Attacks

John Kaminski

John Kaminski is the author of America's Autopsy Report, *a collection of his Internet essays concerning conspiracies allegedly perpetrated by big business, government, and the media.*

The September 11, 2001, attacks on the World Trade Center and Pentagon were among the greatest crimes in American history. Yet the Bush administration has issued dozens of lies about the attack that defy rational analysis. For example, officials first denied that they had any foreknowledge of the planned attacks, but hours later they were somehow able to release the names of the alleged perpetrators. Such inconsistencies are among dozens that have led numerous people to conclude that officials at the highest levels of government were behind the attacks. These treasonous attacks were executed by those who wished to loot the treasury, wage wars based on lies, and institute a dictatorial system. The American people must demand that their political representatives ask hard questions of those in government and big business who had the most to benefit from the 9/11 attacks. The very future of American democracy is at stake.

To most Americans, the first inkling that something was wrong with the official story of the 9/11 catastrophe occurred about a year after the event, when President [George

John Kaminski, "9-11 Cover Up Is Falling Apart," www.abovetopsecret.com, December 21, 2003. Copyright © 2003 by John L. Kaminski. Reproduced by permission.

W.] Bush resisted setting up a panel to investigate the events of that dark day.

Why would he not want to investigate the greatest crime in American history? many wondered. Then, he badly underfunded it. Then, he tried to name infamous power broker [and former secretary of state] Henry Kissinger to head it. Since then, Bush has stonewalled a committee of his own choosing [the National Commission on Terrorist Attacks upon the United States or the Kean Commission] one stacked with political functionaries that is ill-equipped to conduct either a police or forensic investigation and, perhaps most revealing, one that accepted the government's version of who the guilty parties were before they examined any evidence!

To date [December 2003], there has never been anything revealed to the public about how the U.S. government KNOWS that Osama bin Laden and al-Qaeda were the actual perpetrators of 9/11.

Today, millions of Americans realize simply from watching thousands of cop shows on TV that the one most interested in covering up a crime is the one most likely to have committed it. Many more millions also realize that the foremost beneficiaries of the attacks and mass killings of 9/11 are the same people who are now waging wars that are based on some very suspicious rationalizations, most of which since have been exposed as outright lies.

Shockingly enough, even Thomas Kean, chairman of the committee constructed to cover up this greatest crime in American history, blew the whistle the other day that the attacks could have been prevented. Whether this will develop into a real investigation . . . remains to be seen. But Kean's comment was evidence that a much larger percentage of the American people is beginning to sense that the "they hate our freedom" rationale uttered by the president is clearly bogus, and there is much more than meets the media eye happening about 9/11.

To a far smaller number of Americans, the official 9/11 story began to smell much earlier than when Bush tried to stall the official investigation.

Government Lies

When top Bush administration officials immediately and in unison denied knowing that jetliners could be used to attack American landmarks right after 9/11, a number of alert reporters immediately pointed out that this very subject had been under government study for almost a decade. And when U.S. officials immediately released a list of the alleged hijackers, the lie was immediately visible to those with eyes to see: how could they deny knowing this possibility of a massive jetliner attack existed, yet be able to name the alleged hijackers almost instantly because these individuals had been under surveillance for months?

If they could name the alleged hijackers, then they couldn't deny knowing the possibility of using planes as weapons existed, could they?

To date [December 2003], there has never been anything revealed to the public about how the U.S. government KNOWS that Osama bin Laden and al-Qaeda were the actual perpetrators of 9/11.

As astonishing events unfolded after the tragedy the hasty passage of the Patriot Act (approved by Congress despite virtually no one in Congress reading it before voting for it), which nullified large portions of the U.S. Constitution; constant "terror alerts" about which no evidence was ever produced; the war against Afghanistan which was claimed to be a response to 9/11 yet was planned long before 9/11; and the war against Iraq, which was waged because that nation supposedly threatened America with weapons of mass destruction (which have never and will never be found, unless planted) and had ties to that mystery terror group called al-Qaeda (since proven to be lies) many more millions of Americans began to understand that the new peril they were in was not from some shadowy worldwide terror group but from unscrupulous demagogues in Washington who would invent any story and kill any number of people in order to improve the fortunes of the very military/industrial power brokers who illegally brought them to power in the first place.

In the mind of these many more millions of Americans, a new syllogism began to take shape: If they lied about why they went to war in Afghanistan and they lied about why they went to war in Iraq, how stupid would Americans have to be to believe what they said about 9/11?

And yet, through two years of intense flag waving, during which most Americans were too terrified to say anything critical of those who were ostensibly protecting us from this new wave of worldwide terror, the lies became cast in stone. The media, owned by the same shameful specimens who own the weapons making companies, refused to even entertain the notion that the U.S. government could tell blatant lies to its own people, never mind murder thousands of them in one day.

The Jeopardy We Are In

Worse, what passed for the political opposition was afraid to even whisper what was becoming obvious in the minds of so many Americans with functioning brains that the initial signs of a deliberate air defense standdown, the phony mythology about Muslim hijackers, the funny way all those buildings in New York happened to fall, the tiny hole in the Pentagon that was supposedly caused by a giant airliner, and the curiously comatose behavior of our president when the nation he was supposed to be leading was under dire attack that 9/11 bore a multitude of evidential suggestions that it was an inside job, executed to give right-wing crazies a better shot at looting the treasury of their own country in a variety of ways. This scenario has now obviously come to pass.

13

And that is really where we stand today. Shockingly, while millions around the country and billions more around the world are certain that this is what happened, not a single major politician ... has uttered even a single syllable that these millions of Americans who believe something is very wrong that the official 9/11 story just might be right.

If they lied about why they went to war in Afghanistan and they lied about why they went to war in Iraq, how stupid would Americans have to be to believe what they said about 9/11?

And in the so-called American free press, our prostituted media continue a total blackout on the subject, as evidenced by the total silence that accompanied the recent filing of a lawsuit by 9/11 widow Ellen Mariani against President Bush for obstruction of justice and treason.

This is a travesty of mind-boggling proportions. Like the entire Congress that goosestepped late at night while it knocked over the U.S. Constitution, here we have the complete political spectrum every single rich man who has declared his intention to run for president not daring to admit what millions of Americans know beyond doubt in the sincerest depths of their hearts that 9/11 was conceived, devised, planned and carried out from the offices of power in the United States, principally Washington, but also New York and Langley, Virginia, and quite possibly Tel Aviv.

You have only to look at the psychologically palsied and putrescent behavior of the official 9/11 investigative body, the Kean commission as well as the insane and demonic actions of every single functionary in the Bush Administration to know in your heart that it's true.

And realize the jeopardy we are all in.

Bringing Deceptions to Light

Fortunately, there are many scrupulous personalities who haven't bought the shallow lies and who have worked doggedly since that dark day to bring the cynical deceptions to light.

They have analyzed the fall of the WTC [World Trade Center] towers and concluded they were most likely demolished. Why else would so much of the rubble have turned to powder and the towers themselves exploded at the top? Why else would WTC7 [a smaller skyscraper known as World Trade Center Building 7] have fallen in the same manner as the others when it was not hit by a plane?

They have talked the Pentagon scenario to death and concluded there was no legitimate trace of jetliner rubble to be found, written that a hole of that small type was most likely made by a missile, and concluded that reports of identifying the DNA of every passenger on Flight 77 in that rubble was simply an impossible lie if the fires were hot enough to have melted virtually every trace of the crashed airliner.

9/11 was conceived, devised, planned and carried out from the offices of power in the United States, principally Washington, but also New York and Langley, Virginia, and quite possibly Tel Aviv.

They have concluded beyond doubt that the alleged maneuvers of the Pentagon jet could never have been accomplished by someone who did not do well in a small plane at a jerkwater flight school. . . .

That there is so much evidence to convince you that 9/11 was an inside job, that our leading officials are criminals and mass murderers, that you, as a functioning human being on this earth, have no choice but to try to convince your neighbor that something must be done if we are not to go quietly into this police state prison that has been prepared for us.

15

Ways to Solve the Crime

And yet, with all the comprehensive and inspired research that has been done (really, the Kean commission only needs to read the internet before recommending mass arrests for virtually all of the American government's leadership) there are two glaring areas that continue to delay the search for justice about 9/11.

The first involves the suspicious investments prior to 9/11, in which millions of dollars were made by betting the price of certain airline stocks (and other companies, some of which were located in the WTC towers) would go down. Financial laws guarantee a degree of confidentiality in these transactions, even those these laws principally protect crooks with large amounts of money who are often doing something the law does not permit. Nevertheless, the laws are set up to protect these identities.

It stands to reason, just on the basis of rules established in all those TV detective shows, that the powers that be are the ones who committed these heinous crimes.

Had America a great and honest leader, he (or she) would suspend these laws and name the beneficiaries of these suspicious transactions, reasoning that the greater good was served by tracking down the real perpetrators of the 9/11 mass murder instead of protecting the identities who clearly knew that 9/11 was going to happen before it did happen. Could there be any clearer path to uncovering the real criminals who killed all those people in New York and Washington (and later in Afghanistan and Iraq)? No, there couldn't. Any genuine investigation into the crimes of 9/11 would start (and quite possibly finish) right here.

In addition to releasing the contents of the black boxes that were found in the wreckages of the three disaster venues of 9/11, as well as the contents of the footage taken by the confiscated security cameras near the Pentagon (which could clearly reveal what actually did hit the Pentagon), the names of the investors who profited from insider trading in the days prior to 9/11 would give us a clear look at who the actual perpetrators of this unspeakable crime actually were.

It is a way to solve the crime, and it is clear. Logical people must assume that those who would prevent this method of solving this crime clearly have some involvement in it. This is beyond debate.

Israeli Involvement

The second area most researchers have failed to make any real headway in is the involvement of Israel and its intelligence agency the Mossad in the planning and carrying out of the 9/11 attacks. Sure, Israel was one of those many countries that gave advance warning to the U.S. that something like this was about to happen (you remember, those warnings that Bush and his thugs insist they never got, but fortunately were reliably recorded by the other countries themselves).

The facts are that the evidence for Israeli involvement is substantial. Two workers in an Israeli company located in New York got advance warnings by e-mail two hours before the attacks. Israeli "art students" were shadowing the alleged hijackers for many months during their sojourns in flight schools around the United States. Five Israelis were arrested for dancing in celebration shortly after the planes hit the towers; two had connections to the Mossad. And, perhaps foremost, in the city with the largest Jewish population in the entire world, virtually no Israelis were killed in the 9/11 attacks.

Taken together, these coincidences are too astonishing to ignore. And given Israel's history of "false flag" operations (conducting terror and getting the blame shifted to another country), its involvement throughout history in attacks on its own citizens and Jews around the world to get them to behave

17

in a certain way, its ponderous influence on the American congress and the American media, and the words of former Israeli prime minister [Benjamin] Netanyahu, who immediately after the attacks said they were a very good thing for Israel, many millions of people believe that Israel was really the driving force behind 9/11, simply to get the Americans to continue to do their bidding in the Middle East, which as you can see by subsequent events, clearly is continuing to happen.

The withholding of information by the U.S. Securities and Exchange Commission of the names of the men who profited from the suspicious trades in the days before 9/11, and the hidden role of Israeli intelligence in a caper in the biggest Jewish city in the world in a complex owned by Jewish businessmen continue to be the two most significant uninvestigated aspects of 9/11, and the ones most likely to lead to a genuine finding of fact about what really happened on this tragic and significant day.

Unfortunately, the powers that be are doing everything they can to impede investigation into these two areas, as well as into all other areas of information about 9/11.

Thus, it stands to reason, just on the basis of rules established in all those TV detective shows, that the powers that be are the ones who committed these heinous crimes, for the purpose of regimenting society more to their liking, because a regimented society is more profitable, and those under the thumb of a totalitarian capitalist dictatorship, as we are now, are far less likely to solve crimes and discover the perpetrators of the horror of 9/11 that changed the fundamental nature of the nation and the world in which we live.

2

Al Qaeda Terrorists Were Behind the September 11 Attacks

George W. Bush

George W. Bush is the president of the United States. Nine days after the September 11, 2001, attacks, he made this televised address to Congress and the American people.

The United States has become the victim of attacks organized and carried out by the al Qaeda terrorist network. This organization, led by Osama bin Laden, hates America's democratic government, freedom of speech, and freedom of religion. Al Qaeda wants to destroy the American way of life and instill fear in U.S. citizens by carrying out attacks such as the ones on the World Trade Center and Pentagon on September 11, 2001. However, al Qaeda will not prevail. The United States will defend itself and eradicate all terrorist networks. Many nations are joining the United States in this fight to preserve freedom and tolerance.

On September the 11th, enemies of freedom committed an act of war against our country. Americans have known wars—but for the past 136 years, they have been wars on foreign soil, except for one Sunday in 1941. Americans have known the casualties of war—but not at the center of a great city on a peaceful morning. Americans have known surprise attacks—but never before on thousands of civilians. All of this was brought upon us in a single day—and night fell on a different world, a world where freedom itself is under attack.

George W. Bush, address to a joint session of Congress and the American people, September 20, 2001.

Americans have many questions tonight. Americans are asking: Who attacked our country? The evidence we have gathered all points to a collection of loosely affiliated terrorist organizations known as al Qaeda. They are the same murderers indicted for bombing American embassies in Tanzania and Kenya, and responsible for bombing the USS *Cole.*

Al Qaeda is to terror what the mafia is to crime. But its goal is not making money; its goal is remaking the world—and imposing its radical beliefs on people everywhere.

The terrorists practice a fringe form of Islamic extremism that has been rejected by Muslim scholars and the vast majority of Muslim clerics—a fringe movement that perverts the peaceful teachings of Islam. The terrorists' directive commands them to kill Christians and Jews, to kill all Americans, and make no distinction among military and civilians, including women and children.

This group and its leader—a person named Osama bin Laden—are linked to many other organizations in different countries, including the Egyptian Islamic Jihad and the Islamic Movement of Uzbekistan. There are thousands of these terrorists in more than 60 countries. They are recruited from their own nations and neighborhoods and brought to camps in places like Afghanistan, where they are trained in the tactics of terror. They are sent back to their homes or sent to hide in countries around the world to plot evil and destruction.

Demands to the Taliban

The leadership of al Qaeda has great influence in Afghanistan and supports the Taliban regime in controlling most of that country. In Afghanistan, we see al Qaeda's vision for the world.

Afghanistan's people have been brutalized—many are starving and many have fled. Women are not allowed to attend school. You can be jailed for owning a television. Religion can be practiced only as their leaders dictate. A man can be jailed in Afghanistan if his beard is not long enough.

The United States respects the people of Afghanistan—after all, we are currently its largest source of humanitarian aid—but we condemn the Taliban regime. It is not only repressing its own people, it is threatening people everywhere by sponsoring and sheltering and supplying terrorists. By aiding and abetting murder, the Taliban regime is committing murder.

On September the 11th, enemies of freedom committed an act of war against our country.

And tonight, the United States of America makes the following demands on the Taliban: Deliver to United States authorities all the leaders of al Qaeda who hide in your land. Release all foreign nationals, including American citizens, you have unjustly imprisoned. Protect foreign journalists, diplomats and aid workers in your country. Close immediately and permanently every terrorist training camp in Afghanistan, and hand over every terrorist, and every person in their support structure, to appropriate authorities. Give the United States full access to terrorist training camps, so we can make sure they are no longer operating.

These demands are not open to negotiation or discussion. The Taliban must act, and act immediately. They will hand over the terrorists, or they will share in their fate.

America's Enemy

I also want to speak tonight directly to Muslims throughout the world. We respect your faith. It's practiced freely by many millions of Americans, and by millions more in countries that America counts as friends. Its teachings are good and peaceful, and those who commit evil in the name of Allah blaspheme the name of Allah. The terrorists are traitors to their own faith, trying, in effect, to hijack Islam itself. The enemy of America is not our many Muslim friends; it is not our many

Arab friends. Our enemy is a radical network of terrorists, and every government that supports them.

Our war on terror begins with al Qaeda, but it does not end there. It will not end until every terrorist group of global reach has been found, stopped and defeated.

Americans are asking, why do they hate us? They hate what we see right here in this chamber—a democratically elected government. Their leaders are self-appointed. They hate our freedoms—our freedom of religion, our freedom of speech, our freedom to vote and assemble and disagree with each other.

The [al Qaeda] terrorists are traitors to their own faith, trying, in effect, to hijack Islam itself.

They want to overthrow existing governments in many Muslim countries, such as Egypt, Saudi Arabia, and Jordan. They want to drive Israel out of the Middle East. They want to drive Christians and Jews out of vast regions of Asia and Africa.

These terrorists kill not merely to end lives, but to disrupt and end a way of life. With every atrocity, they hope that America grows fearful, retreating from the world and forsaking our friends. They stand against us, because we stand in their way.

We are not deceived by their pretenses to piety. We have seen their kind before. They are the heirs of all the murderous ideologies of the 20th century. By sacrificing human life to serve their radical visions—by abandoning every value except the will to power—they follow in the path of fascism, and Nazism, and totalitarianism. And they will follow that path all the way, to where it ends: in history's unmarked grave of discarded lies.

A Plan for War

Americans are asking: How will we fight and win this war? We will direct every resource at our command—every means of diplomacy, every tool of intelligence, every instrument of law enforcement, every financial influence, and every necessary weapon of war—to the disruption and to the defeat of the global terror network.

This war will not be like the war against Iraq a decade ago, with a decisive liberation of territory and a swift conclusion. It will not look like the air war above Kosovo two years ago [1999], where no ground troops were used and not a single American was lost in combat.

Terrorists attacked a symbol of American prosperity. They did not touch its source.

Our response involves far more than instant retaliation and isolated strikes. Americans should not expect one battle, but a lengthy campaign, unlike any other we have ever seen. It may include dramatic strikes, visible on TV, and covert operations, secret even in success. We will starve terrorists of funding, turn them one against another, drive them from place to place, until there is no refuge or no rest. And we will pursue nations that provide aid or safe haven to terrorism. Every nation, in every region, now has a decision to make. Either you are with us, or you are with the terrorists. From this day forward, any nation that continues to harbor or support terrorism will be regarded by the United States as a hostile regime.

Our nation has been put on notice: We are not immune from attack. We will take defensive measures against terrorism to protect Americans. Today, dozens of federal departments and agencies, as well as state and local governments, have responsibilities affecting homeland security. These efforts must be coordinated at the highest level. So tonight I announce the

creation of a Cabinet-level position reporting directly to me—
the Office of Homeland Security.

And tonight I also announce a distinguished American to
lead this effort, to strengthen American security: a military
veteran, an effective governor, a true patriot, a trusted friend—
Pennsylvania's Tom Ridge. He will lead, oversee and coordi-
nate a comprehensive national strategy to safeguard our country against terrorism, and respond to any attacks that may
come.

These measures are essential. But the only way to defeat
terrorism as a threat to our way of life is to stop it, eliminate
it, and destroy it where it grows.

Many will be involved in this effort, from FBI agents to intelligence operatives to the reservists we have called to active
duty. All deserve our thanks, and all have our prayers. And tonight, a few miles from the damaged Pentagon, I have a mes-
sage for our military: Be ready. I've called the Armed Forces to
alert, and there is a reason. The hour is coming when America
will act, and you will make us proud.

Freedom at Stake

This is not, however, just America's fight. And what is at stake
is not just America's freedom. This is the world's fight. This is
civilization's fight. This is the fight of all who believe in
progress and pluralism, tolerance and freedom.

We ask every nation to join us. We will ask, and we will
need, the help of police forces, intelligence services, and bank-
ing systems around the world. The United States is grateful
that many nations and many international organizations have
already responded—with sympathy and with support. Nations
from Latin America, to Asia, to Africa, to Europe, to the Islamic world. Perhaps the NATO Charter reflects best the atti-
tude of the world: An attack on one is an attack on all.

The civilized world is rallying to America's side. They understand that if this terror goes unpunished, their own cities,

their own citizens may be next. Terror, unanswered, can not only bring down buildings, it can threaten the stability of legitimate governments. And you know what—we're not going to allow it.

What Americans Must Do

Americans are asking: What is expected of us? I ask you to live your lives, and hug your children. I know many citizens have fears tonight, and I ask you to be calm and resolute, even in the face of a continuing threat.

I ask you to uphold the values of America, and remember why so many have come here. We are in a fight for our principles, and our first responsibility is to live by them. No one should be singled out for unfair treatment or unkind words because of their ethnic background or religious faith.

I ask you to continue to support the victims of this tragedy with your contributions. Those who want to give can go to a central source of information, libertyunites.org, to find the names of groups providing direct help in New York, Pennsylvania, and Virginia.

The thousands of FBI agents who are now at work in this investigation may need your cooperation, and I ask you to give it.

I ask for your patience, with the delays and inconveniences that may accompany tighter security; and for your patience in what will be a long struggle.

I ask your continued participation and confidence in the American economy. Terrorists attacked a symbol of American prosperity. They did not touch its source. America is successful because of the hard work, and creativity, and enterprise of our people. These were the true strengths of our economy before September 11th, and they are our strengths today.

And, finally, please continue praying for the victims of terror and their families, for those in uniform, and for our great country. Prayer has comforted us in sorrow, and will help strengthen us for the journey ahead.

A Call to Unite

Tonight I thank my fellow Americans for what you have already done and for what you will do. And ladies and gentlemen of the Congress, I thank you, their representatives, for what you have already done and for what we will do together.

Tonight, we face new and sudden national challenges. We will come together to improve air safety, to dramatically expand the number of air marshals on domestic flights, and take new measures to prevent hijacking. We will come together to promote stability and keep our airlines flying, with direct assistance during this emergency.

We will come together to give law enforcement the additional tools it needs to track down terror here at home. We will come together to strengthen our intelligence capabilities to know the plans of terrorists before they act, and find them before they strike.

We will come together to take active steps that strengthen America's economy, and put our people back to work.

Tonight we welcome two leaders who embody the extraordinary spirit of all New Yorkers: Governor George Pataki, and Mayor Rudolph Giuliani. As a symbol of America's resolve, my administration will work with Congress, and these two leaders, to show the world that we will rebuild New York City.

America Will Prevail

After all that has just passed—all the lives taken, and all the possibilities and hopes that died with them—it is natural to wonder if America's future is one of fear. Some speak of an age of terror. I know there are struggles ahead, and dangers to face. But this country will define our times, not be defined by them. As long as the United States of America is determined and strong, this will not be an age of terror; this will be an age of liberty, here and across the world.

Great harm has been done to us. We have suffered great loss. And in our grief and anger we have found our mission and our moment. Freedom and fear are at war. The advance of human freedom—the great achievement of our time, and the great hope of every time—now depends on us. Our nation—this generation—will lift a dark threat of violence from our people and our future. We will rally the world to this cause by our efforts, by our courage. We will not tire, we will not falter, and we will not fail.

It is my hope that in the months and years ahead, life will return almost to normal. We'll go back to our lives and routines, and that is good. Even grief recedes with time and grace. But our resolve must not pass. Each of us will remember what happened that day, and to whom it happened. We'll remember the moment the news came—where we were and what we were doing. Some will remember an image of a fire, or a story of rescue. Some will carry memories of a face and a voice gone forever.

And I will carry this: It is the police shield of a man named George Howard, who died at the World Trade Center trying to save others. It was given to me by his mom, Arlene, as a proud memorial to her son. This is my reminder of lives that ended, and a task that does not end.

I will not forget this wound to our country or those who inflicted it. I will not yield; I will not rest; I will not relent in waging this struggle for freedom and security for the American people.

The course of this conflict is not known, yet its outcome is certain. Freedom and fear, justice and cruelty, have always been at war, and we know that God is not neutral between them.

Fellow citizens, we'll meet violence with patient justice—assured of the rightness of our cause, and confident of the victories to come. In all that lies before us, may God grant us wisdom, and may He watch over the United States of America.

3

The U.S. Government Developed the AIDS Virus

Alan Cantwell Jr.

Alan Cantwell Jr. is a retired dermatologist and AIDS and cancer researcher who has written extensively about what he considers the man-made development of AIDS.

There is well-documented evidence that in the mid-1970s, weapons researchers working for the U.S. government created viruses remarkably similar to AIDS. These viruses, developed as biological weapons, were transferred to monkeys, cats, and other laboratory animals. Later, the disease was transferred to young gay men and African Americans in Manhattan, Los Angeles, and San Francisco by way of an experimental hepatitis B inoculation program in which subjects were given vaccinations tainted with AIDS. Even as thousands of people were tragically struck down by the man-made disease, scientists and politicians blamed the outbreak on the promiscuous sexual practices of the afflicted groups. There has been virtually no examination of the roles played by government scientists who unleashed the AIDS epidemic on the world. With the media refusing to investigate the origins of AIDS within top-secret bioweapons laboratories, most of the world will never become aware of the conspiracy that started a global plague.

Alan Cantwell Jr., "The Man-Made Origin of AIDS: Are Human and Viral Experiments Responsible for Unleashing the HIV Holocaust?" www.rense.com, November 21, 2003. Copyright © 2003 by Alan Cantwell. Alan Cantwell MD is the author of two books on the man-made origin of AIDS: *AIDS and the Doctors of Death* and *Queer Blood,* both available at www.amazon.com and through Book Clearing House, (800) 431-1579. Web site: www.ariesrisingpress.com.

AIDS in America rarely makes headlines anymore. In the mind of the public the disease is still believed to be a sexually-transmitted disease mostly affecting male homosexuals, drug addicts, prostitutes and promiscuous people. Starting officially in June 1981 as a "gay disease" affecting only a few dozen men, there are now 800,000 reported U.S. AIDS cases and 460,000 deaths, mostly young men. The prediction of a "major threat" to the "general" heterosexual population never happened.

Every December 1, we commemorate World AIDS Day. This year (2003) there are 36 million people worldwide estimated to be living with AIDS/HIV. Twenty-two million people have died of the disease. . . .

The media and the AIDS scientists have never told the real history of AIDS and its origin to the world public. We are repeatedly told that HIV came from Africa. But how is that sexually and biologically possible? How could a supposedly black African heterosexual disease—that some scientists claim has been around for decades or centuries in Africa—suddenly transform itself into an exclusively white male homosexual disease in America, and at a time when AIDS was unknown in Africa?

Is AIDS, in reality, a man-made disease originally produced by human experimentation or human error? Could the bio-engineering of dangerous viruses that preceded the "gay plague" be responsible for the origin of AIDS? In view of covert and unethical government-sponsored human radiation experiments that preceded AIDS, is it fair to blame gays, blacks and chimpanzees for a disease that could have been started by vaccine programs utilizing gays and blacks as guinea-pigs?

These are historical issues that will never be considered by the media. . . . However, there is strong evidence to suggest that HIV/AIDS is indeed a man-made disease, and it is time to "rewrite history" to include long-forgotten and suppressed facts about AIDS and its origin.

Deliberately Introduced

Since the beginning of the AIDS epidemic there have been persistent rumors that the disease was man-made, and that HIV was deliberately "introduced" into the American gay and the African black populations as a germ warfare experiment. This so-called conspiracy theory was quickly squelched by virologists and molecular biologists, who blamed primates in the African bush and human sexuality for the introduction and spread of HIV. In the fall of 1986 the Soviets shocked the world by claiming that HIV was secretly developed at Fort Detrick, the U.S. Army's biological warfare unit. Although the claim was dismissed as "infectious propaganda", Russian scientists had worked hand in hand with biological warfare scientists in the transfer of viruses and virus-infected tissue into various non-human primates (monkeys, apes, chimps) during the 1970s before AIDS appeared. With improved international relationships, the Russian accusation vanished.

Although evidence supporting the man-made theory has never been mentioned in the major U.S. media, the theory continues to be ridiculed. For example, in the *San Francisco Chronicle* ("Quest for the Origin of AIDS", January 14, 2001), William Carlsen writes: "In the early years of the AIDS epidemic, theories attempting to explain the origin of the disease ranged from the comic to the bizarre: a deadly germ escaped from a secret CIA laboratory; God sent the plague down to punish homosexuals and drug addicts; it came from outer space, riding on the tail of a comet."

AIDS certainly did not come from the hand of God or outer space. However, there is ample evidence to suspect the hand of man in the outbreak of AIDS that first began in the late 1970s in New York City.

Creating AIDS in Animals

Lost in the history of AIDS is evidence pointing to HIV as a virus whose origin traces back to animal cancer retrovirus experimentation in the "pre-AIDS" years of the 1960s and 70s. Evidence linking the introduction of HIV into gays and blacks via vaccine experiments and programs in the late 1970s has been totally ignored in favor of the politically correct theory claiming that HIV originated in chimpanzees in the African rain forest, and that HIV "jumped species" into the African population around 1930 or even earlier.

Conveniently overlooked is the series of outbreaks of AIDS-like epidemics that broke out in U.S. primate centers, beginning in 1969. A decade before AIDS, the first of five recorded epidemics of "simian AIDS" erupted in a colony of stump-tailed macaques housed in a primate lab at Davis, California. Most of the macaques died. Two types of primate immunodeficiency viruses were eventually discovered as the cause. A few silently infected monkeys transferred to the primate colony at Yerkes [research facility] in Atlanta subsequently died of simian AIDS in the late 1980s. Veterinarians claim the origin of the simian AIDS outbreak is unknown. However, one obvious possibility is the experimental transfer of viruses between various primate species, which is common practice in animal laboratories.

In the fall of 1986 the Soviets shocked the world by claiming that HIV was secretly developed at Fort Detrick, the U.S. Army's biological warfare unit.

In 1974 veterinarians actually created an AIDS-like disease when newborn chimps were removed from their mothers and weaned exclusively on virus-infected milk from cows infected with "bovine C-type virus." Within a year the chimps died of leukemia and pneumocystis pneumonia (the "gay pneumonia" of AIDS). Both diseases had never been observed in chimps before this virus-transfer experiment.

Also downplayed is the laboratory creation of feline leukemia and 'cat AIDS' by the transfer of HIV-like cat retroviruses in the mid-1970s. These experiments were conducted at Harvard by Myron (Max) Essex, later to become a famous AIDS researcher. All this man-made creation of AIDS in laboratory animals directly preceded the "mysterious" 1979 introduction of HIV into gay men, the most hated minority in America.

Nowadays, scientists hunt for "ancestor" viruses of HIV in chimps in the African wild and ignore all the immunosuppressive viruses that were created in virus laboratories shortly before AIDS. No consideration is given to any of these lab viruses as possible man-made ancestors of the many "strains" of HIV (and HIV-2) that jumped species to produce AIDS in humans.

The Gay Experiments That Preceded AIDS (1978–1981)

Scientists also discount any connection between the official outbreak of AIDS in 1981 and the experimental hepatitis B vaccine program (1978–1981) at the New York Blood Center in Manhattan that used gays as guinea pigs shortly before the epidemic. Curiously, the exact origin of AIDS in the United States remains unstudied. Health authorities simply blame promiscuous gay men, but never adequately explain how a black heterosexual African disease could have transformed itself exclusively into a white young gay male disease in Manhattan.

Researchers claim HIV incubated in Africa for more that a half century until AIDS broke out there in 1982. However, in the U.S. there was no incubation period for gay men. As soon as homosexuals signed up as guinea pigs for government-sponsored hepatitis B vaccine experiments, they began to die with a strange virus of unknown origin. The hepatitis B experiments began in Manhattan in the fall of 1978; the first few cases of AIDS (all young gays from Manhattan) were reported to the CDC [Centers for Disease Control] in 1979.

Scientists have also failed to explain how a brand-new herpes virus was also introduced exclusively into gays, along with HIV, in the late 1970s. This herpes virus is now believed to be the cause of Kaposi's sarcoma, the so-called "gay cancer" of AIDS. Before AIDS, Kaposi's sarcoma was never seen in healthy young men. Identified a decade after HIV, in 1994, this KS virus is closely related to a primate cancer-causing herpes virus extensively studied and transferred in animal laboratories in the decade before AIDS.

Also downplayed to the public is a new microbe (Mycoplasma penetrans), also of unknown origin, that was introduced into homosexuals, along with HIV and the new herpes virus. Thus, not one but three new infectious agents were inexplicably transferred into the gay population at the start of the epidemic (HIV, the herpes KS virus, and M.penetrans).

There is ample evidence to suspect the hand of man in the outbreak of AIDS that first began in the late 1970s in New York City.

In his book, *Virus,* Luc Montagnier (the French virologist who codiscovered HIV) blames promiscuous American gay tourists for bringing this new mycoplasma to Africa, and for bringing back HIV. He provides no evidence for this homophobic theory. Nor does he mention the various mycoplasmas that were passed around in the 1970s in scientific labs, and the fact that these microbes were frequent contaminants in virus cultures and vaccines.

Why are all these simultaneous introductions of new infectious agents into gay men ignored by scientists? Surely a credible explanation would be important in determining the origin of HIV and AIDS.

Why are scientists so opposed to the man-made theory? And why do they believe so passionately in the chimp theory? One explanation might be that scientists don't want the public to know what happened to the tens of thousands of imported primates who were held captive in laboratories throughout the world in the decade before AIDS.

The Forgotten Special Virus Cancer Program (1964–1977)

Rarely mentioned by AIDS scientists and media reporters is the fact that surgeons have been transplanting chimpanzee parts (and chimp viruses) into people for decades. When Keith Reemtsma died in June 2000, at age 74, he was hailed as a pioneer in cross-species organ transplants (now known as xenotransplantation). By 1964 he had already placed six chimpanzee kidneys into six patients. All his patients died, but eventually Reemtsma succeeded in many successful human-to-human organ transplants.

Much more likely to have spread primate (chimp and monkey) viruses to human beings is the largely forgotten Special Virus Cancer Program (SVCP). This research program was responsible for the development, the production, the seeding, and the deployment of various animal cancer and immunosuppressive AIDS-like viruses and retroviruses. These laboratory created viruses were capable of inducing disease when transferred between animal species and also when transplanted into human cells and tissue.

Man-made creation of AIDS in laboratory animals directly preceded the "mysterious" 1979 introduction of HIV into gay men, the most hated minority in America.

The SVCP began in 1964 as a government-funded program of the National Cancer Institute (NCI) in Bethesda, Maryland. Originally designed to study leukemia, the program was soon enlarged to study all forms of cancer. The scope of the program was international and included scientists from Japan, Sweden, Italy, the Netherlands, Israel, and Africa. The mission of the SVCP was to collect various human and animal cancers from around the world and to grow large amounts of cancer-causing viruses. As a result, thousands of liters of dangerous man-made viruses were adapted to human cells and shipped around the world to various laboratories. The annual reports of the SVCP contain proof that species jumping of animal viruses was a common occurrence in labs a decade before AIDS.

The SVCP gathered together the nation's top virologists, biochemists, immunologists, molecular biologists, and epidemiologists, to determine the role of viruses and retroviruses in the production of human cancer. Many of the most prestigious medical institutions were involved in this program.

Connected with the SVCP were the most famous future American AIDS scientists, such as Robert Gallo (the codiscoverer of HIV), Max Essex of "cat AIDS" fame, and Peter Duesberg, who claims HIV does not cause AIDS. Gallo and Essex were also the first to promote the widely accepted African green monkey theory of AIDS.[1] This theory was proven erroneous as far back as 1988, but was heavily circulated among AIDS educators and the media until the theory was superseded by the chimp theory in the late 1990s.

Biowarfare Research, Primate Research, and the SVCP

Also joining forces with the SVCP at the NCI were the military's biological warfare researchers. On October 18, 1971, President Richard Nixon announced that the army's biowarfare laboratories at nearby Fort Detrick, Maryland, would be converted to cancer research. As part of Nixon's so-called War on Cancer, the military biowarfare unit was retitled the new Frederick Cancer Research Center, and Litton Bionetics was named as the military's prime contractor for this project. According to the 1971 SVCP annual report, the primary task of

---

1. In the mid-1980s, Max Essex, a professor at Harvard University, claimed that the AIDS virus had spread to man from the African green monkey (*Cercopithecus aethiops*).

the now jointly connected National Cancer Institute–Frederick Cancer Research Center was "the large scale production of oncogenic (cancer-causing) and suspected oncogenic viruses to meet research needs on a continuing basis." Special attention was given to primate viruses (the alleged African source of HIV) and "the successful propagation of significant amounts of human candidate viruses." Candidate viruses were animal or human viruses that might cause human cancers.

Could virus-contaminated hepatitis vaccines lie at the root of AIDS?

For these experiments a steady supply of research animals (monkeys, chimpanzees, mice, and cats) was necessary; and multiple breeding colonies were established for the SVCP. Primates were shipped in from West Africa and Asia for experimentation; and virus-infected animals were shipped out to various labs worldwide. By 1971, a total of 2,274 primates had been inoculated at Bionetics Research Laboratories, under contract to Fort Detrick. Over 1,000 of these monkeys had already died or had been transferred to other primate centers. (Some animals were eventually released back into the wild.) By the early 1970s, experimenters had transferred cancer-causing viruses into several species of monkeys, and had also isolated a monkey virus (Herpesvirus saimiri) that would have a close genetic relationship to the new Kaposi's sarcoma herpes virus that produced the "gay cancer" of AIDS in 1979.

In order to induce primates and other research animals to acquire cancer, their immune system was deliberately suppressed by drugs, radiation, or cancer-causing chemicals or substances. The thymus gland and/or the spleen were removed, and viruses were injected into newborn animals or into the womb of pregnant animals. Some animals were injected with malaria to keep them chronically sick and immunodepressed. . . .

The End of the SVCP and the Birth of AIDS

By 1977 the SVCP came to an inglorious end. According to Gallo, "Scientifically, the problem was that no one could supply clear evidence of any kind of human tumor virus, not even a DNA virus, and most researchers refused to concede that viruses played any role in human cancers. Politically, the Virus Cancer Program was vulnerable because it attracted a great deal of money and attention and had failed to produce dramatic, visible results."

Despite all this, the SVCP was the birthplace of genetic engineering, molecular biology, and the human genome project. More than any other program it built up the field of animal retrovirology, which led to the vital understanding of cancer and immunosuppressive retroviruses in humans.

As the SVCP was winding down, thousands of gay men were signing up as guinea pigs in government-sponsored hepatitis B vaccine experiments in New York, Los Angeles, and San Francisco. These same cities would soon become the three primary epicenters for the new "gay-related immune deficiency syndrome," later known as AIDS.

Two years after the termination of the SVCP, the introduction of HIV into gay men (along with a herpes virus and a mycoplasma) miraculously revived retroviral research and made Gallo the most famous scientist in the world.

Could virus-contaminated hepatitis vaccines lie at the root of AIDS? In the early 1970s the hepatitis B vaccine was developed in chimpanzees. To this day, some people are fearful about taking the hepatitis B vaccine because of its original connection to gay men and AIDS.

Was HIV (and the KS herpes virus and a new mycoplasma) introduced into gays during these vaccine trials when thousands of homosexuals were injected in Manhattan beginning in 1978, and in the West Coast cities in 1980–1981?

As mentioned, the first gay AIDS cases erupted in Manhattan a few months after the gay experiment began at the NY

Blood Center. When a blood test for HIV became available in the mid-1980s, the Center's stored gay blood specimens were reexamined. Most astonishing is the statistically significant fact that 20% of the gay men who volunteered for the hepatitis B experiment in New York were discovered to be HIV-positive in 1980 (a year before the AIDS epidemic became "official" in 1981). This signifies that Manhattan gays in 1980 had the highest incidence of HIV anywhere in the world, including Africa, the supposed birthplace of HIV and AIDS. And epidemic cases in Africa did not appear until 1982.

Although denied by the AIDS establishment, a few researchers are convinced that these vaccine experiments served as the vehicle through which HIV was introduced into the gay population.

4

The U.S. Government Did Not Develop the AIDS Virus

Earl Ofari Hutchinson

Earl Ofari Hutchinson is a political analyst, editorialist, and author whose books include The Crisis in Black and Black.

Millions of black people believe that government scientists created the AIDS virus to deliberately infect African Americans. There is little evidence to back up this belief, but the AIDS conspiracy theory is, ironically, helping spread the disease. Many of those who believe that the government is responsible for the AIDS epidemic feel that there is nothing that they can do to stop the disease. This feeling of powerlessness makes many people less likely to practice safe sex, get AIDS tests, or take other measures to protect themselves. Black leaders need to speak out against those spreading AIDS conspiracy theories. To do less is to compound the tragedy even as thousands of African Americans contract the disease.

AIDS activists were livid at the findings of a recently released RAND study that found that huge numbers of blacks still believe that the AIDS epidemic in black communities is a genocidal plot to wipe out blacks. The conspirators are, take your pick: secret government labs, the CIA, diabolical scientists and doctors, international health agencies or unnamed forces. The RAND study conducted in conjunction with Oregon State University appeared in the Feb. 1 [2005]

Earl Ofari Hutchinson, "Chasing AIDS Conspiracies," AlterNet, www.alternet.org/story/21127, August 1, 2005.

edition of the *Journal of Acquired Immune Deficiency Syndromes*. It's the most extensive probe yet of AIDS conspiracy theories among blacks.

AIDS activists blame loose and irresponsible talk about AIDS as a reason many blacks resist pleas to get tested and treated, fail to consistently use condoms, and also fail to back AIDS prevention and education programs. That failure has had devastating consequences. Blacks account for more than half of the new AIDS and HIV cases in America. Among black women and young persons, the figures are even more horrific. According to government reports, in 2003, blacks aged 18-to-24 made up four out of five new AIDS cases. Black women made up nearly 3 out of four of new AIDS cases.

AIDS activists blame loose and irresponsible talk about AIDS as a reason many blacks resist pleas to get tested and treated.

Though the RAND study is the most extensive study yet to document AIDS conspiracy notions among blacks, the study did not answer why, despite all scientific and medical evidence to the contrary, this dangerous and deadly racial paranoia is still rampant among so many blacks. Contrary to what many AIDS activists say, this is not solely a cop-out by them to evade personal responsibility for profligate sexual practices or to reject AIDS education programs.

The Conspiracy Bug

The conspiracy bug has long bit many Americans. There are packs of groups that span a political spectrum of extreme rightists, Aryan Nation racists, Millennium Christian fundamentalists, leftist radicals, and fraternal lodges and societies. Their internet sites bristle with purported official documents that detail and expose these alleged plots. These groups and thousands of individuals believe that government, corporate, or international Zionist groups busily hatch secret plots, and concoct hidden plans to wreak havoc on their lives. Hollywood and the TV industry have also horned in on the conspiracy act. They churn out countless movies and TV shows in which shadowy, government groups topple foreign governments, assassinate government leaders, and brainwash operatives to do dirty deeds.

The conspiracy rumblings began almost from the moment that AIDS began to sledgehammer black communities in the 1980s.

The conspiracy bug bit many blacks especially hard beginning in the 1960s. They were convinced that murky government agencies flooded the ghettoes with drugs, alcohol, gangs, and guns to sow division and disunity among black organizations, eliminate militant black leaders, jail black politicians and quash black activism. Their conspiracy fantasies and paranoia was fueled by well-documented spying by Army Intelligence, the Justice Department and the FBI on the Nation of Islam, the Black Panther Party, the NAACP and other black groups, the Tuskegee experiment that stretched from 1932 into the 1970s in which federal officials knowingly withheld curative medical treatment to black men in Alabama infected with syphilis, and the corruption probes that targeted black elected officials in the 1980s.

There has never been any evidence of any organized government plan to commit genocide against blacks.

The jewel in the conspiracy theory crown was the murder of Martin Luther King, Jr. in April 1968. The claim was that King's convicted killer, James Earl Ray was a Lee Harvey Oswald–type[1] patsy and that government spy agencies—most

1. Lee Harvey Oswald killed President John F. Kennedy.

notably the FBI—orchestrated King's murder. In 1997, the King family jumped on the conspiracy bandwagon and demanded that Ray get a new trial presumably to ferret out the racist or government conspirators behind his murder. There has never been any solid proof that the FBI or other government agents killed King. Yet the ferocity of the FBI's secret war against King, and the many questions the FBI probe into his assassination left unanswered created enough of a wedge for many blacks to believe and to continue to shout conspiracy even after Ray's death in 1998. The AIDS conspiracy theories are hardly new either. The conspiracy rumblings began almost from the moment that AIDS began to sledgehammer black communities in the 1980s. Many blacks fingered the same list of usual suspects then as the RAND study documents that they finger today.

Reckless Theories

While government agencies in America have occasionally played fast and loose with the law and even the rules of democracy, and have spied on and harassed black leaders and groups, there has never been any evidence of any organized government plan to commit genocide against blacks. Still, the fervent belief that there is such a plan is just enough to make many blacks panic, circle the wagons and see hidden plots against them everywhere.

If, as AIDS activists claim, and the RAND study at least inferentially seems to confirm, reckless conspiracy theories about the AIDS plague among blacks are a cause of needless deaths and suffering within black communities, black leaders must speak out loudly against them. It's not a matter of racial one-upmanship. It's a matter of saving lives.

5

The CIA Planned John F. Kennedy's Assassination

Steven Hager

Steven Hager is the editor of High Times *magazine and the author of the book* Adventures in the Counterculture, *from which the following article is excerpted.*

When John F. Kennedy was elected in 1960, the youthful president brought a new style of governing to the White House. Kennedy hoped to shun confrontation with America's enemies in the Soviet Union and Cuba and advocated negotiation to maintain peace. Unfortunately, the president's style created deep hostility among certain people within the military, FBI, and CIA. These men conspired to assassinate Kennedy and carried out the deed on November 22, 1963. When it was later discovered that Lee Harvey Oswald, the president's alleged assassin, had ties to far-right-wing groups in New Orleans, the city's district attorney, Jim Garrison, investigated and tried to prosecute Oswald's associates. A successful prosecution of these men would have proved a conspiracy in the Kennedy assassination and invalidated the government's central lie—that Oswald was a "lone nut" who killed the president. Unfortunately, Garrison's case was sabotaged by a massive onslaught of negative press in the national media as well as shadowy agents who infiltrated his office. Although Garrison lost his case in court, many people believe that the young president's death was planned by agents working for conspirators within the federal government.

Although John F. Kennedy was neither a saint nor a great intellectual, he was the youngest President ever elected, which may explain why he was so well attuned to the changing mood of America in the '60s. Americans had grown weary of Cold War hysteria. They wanted to relax and have fun. Like the majority of people across the planet, they wanted peace.

The President's primary obstacle in this quest was a massive, power-hungry bureaucracy which had emerged after WWII—a Frankenstein monster created by anti-Communist paranoia and inflated defense budgets. By 1960, the Pentagon was easily the world's largest corporation, with assets of over $60 billion. No one understood this monster better than President Dwight D. Eisenhower.

On January 17, 1961, in his farewell address to the nation, Eisenhower spoke to the country, and to his successor, John Kennedy. "The conjunction of an immense military establishment and a large arms industry is new in the American experience," said Eisenhower. "We must guard against the acquisition of unwarranted influence, whether sought or unsought, by the military-industrial complex."

Major Crises

At the beginning of his administration, Kennedy seems to have followed the advice of his military and intelligence officers. What else could such an inexperienced President have done? Signs of a serious rift, however, first appeared after the Bay of Pigs, a CIA-planned-and-executed invasion of Cuba which took place three months after Kennedy took office. The invasion was so bungled that Kennedy refused to send American troops to save the day and immediately afterward fired CIA Director Allen Dulles, Deputy Director General Charles Cabell and Deputy Director of Planning Richard Bissell.

Kennedy's next major crisis occurred on October 16, 1962, when he was shown aerial photos of missile bases in Cuba. The Joint Chiefs of Staff pressed for an immediate attack. Instead, Attorney General Robert Kennedy was sent to meet with Soviet Ambassador Anatoly Dobrynin. In his memoirs, Soviet Premier Nikita Khrushchev quotes the younger Kennedy as saying: "The President is in a grave situation. . . . We are under pressure from our military to use force against Cuba. . . . If the situation continues much longer, the President is not sure that the military will not overthrow him and seize power."

[Kennedy's] command to begin the Vietnam withdrawal was his last formal executive order.

Military hopes for an invasion of Cuba evaporated as Khrushchev and Kennedy worked out a nonviolent solution to the crisis. In return, Kennedy promised not to invade Cuba. Angered over the Bay of Pigs fiasco, the CIA refused to bend to Kennedy's will and continued their destabilization campaign against Castro, which included sabotage raids conducted by a secret army, as well as plots against Castro's life, which were undertaken with the help of well-known Mafia figures such as Johnny Roselli, Sam Giancana and Santos Trafficante. A bitter internal struggle developed around Kennedy's attempts to disband the CIA's paramilitary bases in Florida and Louisiana.

On August 5, 1963, the US, Great Britain and the Soviet Union signed a limited nuclear test ban treaty. Engineered by President Kennedy and long in negotiation, the treaty was a severe blow to the Cold Warriors in the Pentagon and the CIA. On September 20, 1963, Kennedy spoke hopefully of peace to the UN General Assembly. "Today we may have reached a pause in the Cold War," he said. "If both sides can now gain new confidence and experience in concrete collaborations of peace, then surely, this first small step can be the start of a long, fruitful journey."

"Years later, paging through its formerly classified records, talking to the National Security Council staff, it is difficult to avoid the impression that the President was learning the responsibility of power," writes John Prados in his book *Keepers of the Keys*, an analysis of the National Security Council. "Here was a smoother, calmer Kennedy, secretly working for rapprochement with Fidel Castro and a withdrawal from Vietnam."

Kennedy and Vietnam

Although Kennedy's Vietnam policy has not received widespread publicity, he turned resolutely against the war in June of 1963, when he ordered Defense Secretary Robert McNamara and Chairman of the Joint Chiefs of Staff General Maxwell Taylor to announce from the White House steps that all American forces would be withdrawn by 1965. At the time, 15,500 US "advisors" were stationed in South Vietnam, and total casualties suffered remained a relatively low 100.

"Those fellows on the Warren Commission were dead wrong. . . .There's no way in the world that one man could have shot up Jack Kennedy that way."

On November 14, Kennedy signed an order to begin the withdrawal by removing 1,000 troops. In private, Kennedy let it be known the military was not going to railroad him into continuing the war. Many of the hard-line anti-Communists—including FBI Director J. Edgar Hoover—would have to be purged. Bobby Kennedy [the attorney general and the president's brother] would be put in charge of dismantling the CIA. President Kennedy told Senator Mike Mansfield of his plans to tear the CIA "into a thousand pieces and scatter it to the wind." But these plans had to wait for Kennedy's reelection in 1964. And in order to win that election, he had to secure the South. Which is why Kennedy went to Texas later that month.

Could John Kennedy have stopped the war in Vietnam, as was his obvious intention? America will never know. His command to begin the Vietnam withdrawal was his last formal executive order. Just after noon on November 22 [1963], President Kennedy was murdered while driving through downtown Dallas, in full view of dozens of ardent supporters, and while surrounded by police and personal bodyguards. . . . Years later, grave doubts still linger about who pulled the triggers, who ordered the assassination, and why our government has done so little to bring justice forth.

In 1963, no American wanted to believe that President Kennedy's death was a coup d'etat, planned by the military establishment and executed by the CIA. Today, such a claim can no longer be dismissed. Why has the national media done such an abysmal job of presenting the facts to the American people? Some light was shed by Oliver Stone's film *JFK*, a $30 million epic starring Kevin Costner, released to coincide with the 30th anniversary of Kennedy's death. As his focal point for the story, Stone chose former New Orleans District Attorney Jim Garrison, the only prosecutor to attempt to bring this case to court, and a man subjected to one of the most effective smear campaigns ever orchestrated by the U.S. government. It is a frightening story of murder, corruption and cover-up. Even today, 35 years after he brought the case to court, a powerful media disinformation campaign against Garrison continues. . . .

A New Orleans Connection?

In 1961, Garrison decided to run for district attorney on a platform openly hostile to then–New Orleans Mayor Victor Schiro. To the surprise of many, he was elected without any major political backing. At 43, he had been district attorney for less than two years when Kennedy was killed. "I was an old-fashioned patriot," he writes in *On the Trail of the Assassins,* "a product of my family, my military experience, and my years in the legal profession. I could not imagine then that the government would ever deceive the citizens of this country."

A few hours after the assassination, Lee Harvey Oswald was arrested. Two days later, while in Dallas police custody, Oswald was murdered by nightclub owner Jack Ruby. Garrison learned that Oswald was from New Orleans, and arranged a Sunday afternoon meeting with his staff. With such an important case, it was their responsibility to investigate Oswald's local connections.

Within days, they learned that Oswald had recently been seen in the company of David Ferrie, a fervent anti-Communist and freelance pilot linked to the Bay of Pigs invasion. Evidence placed Ferrie in Texas on the day of the assassination. Also on that day, a friend of Ferrie's named Guy Bannister had pistol-whipped one Jack Martin during an argument. Martin confided to friends that Bannister and Ferrie were somehow involved in the assassination. Garrison had Ferrie picked up for questioning, and turned him over to the local FBI, who immediately released him. Within a few months, the Warren Commission released its report stating that Oswald was a "lone nut" murdered by a misguided patriot [Jack Ruby] who wanted to spare Jackie Kennedy the ordeal of testifying. Like most Americans, Garrison accepted this conclusion.

"Garrison would subpoena a witness and two days later the witness would be killed by a parked car."

Three years later, in the fall of '66, Garrison was happily married with three children and content with his job, when a chance conversation with Senator Russell Long changed his views on the Warren Commission forever.

"Those fellows on the Warren Commission were dead wrong," said Long. "There's no way in the world that one man could have shot up Jack Kennedy that way."

Intrigued, Garrison went back to his office and ordered the complete 26-volume report. "The mass of information was disorganized and confused," writes Garrison. "Worst of all, the conclusions in the report seemed to be based on an appallingly selective reading of the evidence, ignoring credible testimony from literally dozens of witnesses."

Garrison was equally disturbed by the background of the men chosen by President Johnson to serve on the commission.

Why, for instance, was Allen Dulles, a man fired by Kennedy, on the panel? A master spy during WWII, Dulles had orchestrated surveillance of the Abwehr (Hitler's military intelligence agency). In the final days of the war, he'd supervised the secret surrender of the elite Nazi SS Corps, and he'd also played a major role in the subsequent incorporation of hundreds of Nazi war criminals, scientists and spies into the newly formed CIA. He was powerful, well-connected to Wall Street and had been director of the CIA for eight years. Certainly, he was no friend to John Kennedy.

Serving with Dulles were U.S. Rep. Gerald Ford, a man described by *Newsweek* as "the CIA's best friend in Congress," John McCloy, former assistant secretary of war and commissioner for occupied Germany immediately after the war, and Senator Richard Russell, chairman of the powerful Senate Armed Services Committee. Russell's home state of Georgia was peppered with military bases and military-industrial contracts. The balance of the commission was clearly in the hands of the military and CIA. The entire "investigation" was supervised by J. Edgar Hoover, who openly detested the Kennedy brothers.

Another interesting link turned up: The mayor of Dallas was Earle Cabell, brother of Gen. Charles Cabell, who JFK had earlier fired from the CIA. Earle Cabell was in a position to control many important details involved in the case, including the Dallas police force.

A Highly Secret Investigation

Based on these general suspicions, Garrison launched a highly secret investigation around Lee Harvey Oswald's links to David Ferrie and Guy Bannister. Unfortunately, Bannister had died nine months after the assassination. An alcoholic and rabid right-winger, Bannister had been a former Naval intelligence operative and a star agent for the FBI. He was a member of the CIA-led John Birch Society and the Minutemen, and publisher of a racist newsletter. His office at 544 Camp Street was a well-known meeting place for anti-Castro Cubans.

Ferrie's background was even more bizarre. A former senior pilot for Eastern Airlines, Ferrie had been the head of the New Orleans Civil Air Patrol, an organization Oswald had joined as a teenager. Many of the boys in the Civil Air Patrol willingly had themselves hypnotized by Ferrie, supposedly to improve their skills and ability to withstand pain. Some of them attended homosexual orgies at Ferrie's house. When complaints concerning these parties were filed with the New Orleans police, Ferrie somehow had the investigations quashed, despite rampant evidence of sexual child abuse.

"Some long-cherished illusions about the great free press in our country underwent a painful reappraisal during this period."

Ferrie suffered from alopecia, an ailment that left him hairless. He wore bright red wigs and painted eyebrows. He founded his own religion, and kept hundreds of experimental rats in his house. He reportedly had flown dozens of solo missions for the CIA in Cuba and Latin America, and had links to Carlos Marcello, head of the Mob in Louisiana. Like Bannister, he was extremely right-wing. "I want to train killers," Ferrie had written to the commander of the U.S. Air Force.

"There is nothing I would enjoy better than blowing the hell out of every damn Russian, Communist, Red or what-have-you."

On the day of the assassination, Dean Andrews, a New Orleans attorney, had been asked to fly to Dallas to represent Oswald. When asked by the Warren Commission who had hired him, Andrews had replied Clay Bertrand.

Bertrand, Garrison discovered, was a pseudonym used by Clay Shaw, director of the International Trade Mart. Shaw, a darling of New Orleans high society, was also well connected in international high-finance circles. He was also an associate of Bannister and Ferrie. Like many others connected with the assassination, Shaw was a former Army intelligence operative. The case against Shaw was circumstantial, but Garrison did have an eyewitness willing to testify that Shaw had met with Lee Harvey Oswald just prior to the assassination.

Disruptive Attacks in the Media

Just as Garrison was marshalling his case, some strange events took place. On February 17, 1967, the *New Orleans States-Item* published a story on Garrison's secret probe, indicating he had already spent over $8,000 of taxpayers' money investigating the Kennedy assassination.

Soon thereafter, Garrison received an unusually strong letter of support from a Denver oil businessman named John Miller, hinting that Miller wanted to offer financial support to the investigation. When Miller arrived in New Orleans, he met with Garrison and one of his assistants.

"You're too big for this job," said Miller. "I suggest you accept an appointment to the bench in federal district court, and move into a job worthy of your talents."

"And what would I have to do to get this judgeship?" asked Garrison.

"Stop your investigation," replied Miller calmly.

Garrison asked Miller to leave his office.

"Well, they offered you the carrot and you turned it down," said his assistant. "You know what's coming next, don't you?"

Suddenly, reporters from all over the country descended on New Orleans, including *Washington Post* contributor George Lardner, Jr. At midnight on February 22, 1967, Lardner claims to have conducted a four-hour interview with Ferrie. The following morning, Ferrie was found dead. Two unsigned, typewritten suicide notes were found. One letter made reference to a "messianic district attorney."

Three days later the coroner announced Ferrie had died of natural causes and placed the time of death well before the end of Lardner's supposed marathon interview. Lardner's possible complicity in the affair would never be called into question, while his highly influential articles in the *Washington Post* branded Garrison's investigation a "fraud." It was just the beginning of a long series of disruptive attacks in the media, and the first of many people connected with the case that would mysteriously turn up dead.

With Ferrie gone, Garrison had only one suspect left. He rushed his case to court, arresting Clay Shaw.

Building Up to the Trial

Ellen Ray, a documentary filmmaker from New York, came to New Orleans to film the story. "People were getting killed left and right," she recalls. "Garrison would subpoena a witness and two days later the witness would be killed by a parked car. I thought Garrison was a great American patriot. But things got a little too heavy when I started getting strange phone calls from men with Cuban accents." After several death threats, Ray became so terrified that instead of making a documentary on the trial, she fled the country.

Attorney General Ramsey Clark, a close friend of President Lyndon Johnson, announced from Washington that the federal government had already investigated and exonerated

Clay Shaw. "Needless to say," writes Garrison, "this did not exactly make me look like District Attorney of the Year."

Meanwhile, all sorts of backpedaling was going on at the Justice Department. If Shaw had been investigated, why wasn't his name in the Warren Commission Report? "The Attorney General has since determined that this was erroneous," said a spokesman for Clark. "Nothing arose indicating a need to investigate Mr. Shaw."

The FBI had encouraged many witnesses to alter their testimony to fit the "lone nut" theory.

Realizing he was in a political minefield, Garrison presented his case as cautiously as possible. A grand jury was convened that included Jay C. Albarado. "On March 14, three criminal-court judges heard Garrison's case in a preliminary hearing to determine if there was enough evidence against Shaw to hold him for trial," Albarado wrote many years later in a letter to the *New Orleans Times-Picayune*. "What did they conclude? That there was sufficient evidence. Garrison then presented his evidence to a 12-member grand jury. We ruled there was sufficient evidence to bring Shaw to trial. Were we duped by Garrison? I think not."

Thanks to all the unwanted publicity, Garrison's staff had swollen with volunteers eager to work on the case. The 6'6" Garrison, now dubbed the "Jolly Green Giant," had already become a hero to the many citizens and researchers who had serious doubts about the Warren Commission.

Unfortunately, a few of these eager volunteers were later exposed as government informers. Shortly before the case went to trial, one of the infiltrators copied all of Garrison's files and turned them over to Shaw's defense team.

On September 4, 1967, Supreme Court Chief Justice Earl Warren announced that Garrison's case was worthless. The *New York Times* characterized the investigation as a "morbid frolic." *Newsweek* reported that the conspiracy was "a plot of Garrison's own making." *Life* magazine published the first of many reports linking Garrison with the Mafia. (Richard Billings, an editor at *Life*, had been one of the first journalists to gain access to Garrison's inner circle, under the guise of "wanting to help" the investigation.) Walter Sheridan, a former Naval intelligence operative and NBC investigator, appeared in New Orleans with a film crew. Their purpose? An exposé titled "The Case of Jim Garrison," which was broadcast in June of '67. "It required only a few minutes to see that NBC had classified the case as criminal and had appointed itself as the prosecutor," writes Garrison.

Puzzled by the intensity of NBC's attack, Garrison went to the library and did some research on the company. He learned the network was a subsidiary of RCA, a bulwark of the military-industrial complex whose defense contracts had increased by more than a billion dollars from 1960 to 1967. Its chairman, retired General David Sarnoff, was a well-known proponent of the Cold War.

"Some long-cherished illusions about the great free press in our country underwent a painful reappraisal during this period," writes Garrison.

A Long Shadow of Doubt

Clay Shaw was brought to trial on January 29, 1969. It took less than one month for Garrison to present his case. Demonstrating the cover-up was the easy part. Although the overwhelming majority of eyewitnesses in Dealey Plaza testified that the fatal shot came not from the Texas School Book Depository—where Oswald worked—but from a grassy knoll overlooking the plaza, the FBI had encouraged many witnesses to alter their testimony to fit the "lone nut" theory. Those that didn't were simply ignored by the commission. The ballistic evidence was flawed and obviously tampered with. Even though the FBI had received several warnings of the assassination, they had ignored them. Security for the President was strangely lax. Although Oswald's killer, Jack Ruby, had ties to the CIA and Mafia, this evidence had been suppressed. Ruby was never allowed to testify before the commission. When interviewed in a Texas jail by Chief Justice Warren and Gerald Ford, he told them: "I would like to request that I go to Washington. . . . I want to tell the truth, and I can't tell it here. . . . Gentlemen, my life is in danger." Ruby never made it to Washington. He remained in jail and died mysteriously before Garrison could call him as a witness.

Even more disturbing was the treatment given the deceased President's corpse. Under Texas law, an autopsy should have been performed by a civilian pathologist in Dallas. Instead, the body was removed at gunpoint by the Secret Service and flown to a naval hospital in Maryland, where an incomplete autopsy was performed under the supervision of unnamed admirals and generals. The notes from this "autopsy" were quickly burned. Bullet holes were never tracked, the brain was not dissected and organs were not removed. The autopsy was a botched, tainted affair, performed under military supervision. (The medical aspects of the case were so weird, they would later form the basis for a best-selling book on the assassination, *Best Evidence* by David Lifton.)

The most important and lasting piece of evidence unveiled by Garrison was an 8mm film of the assassination taken by Abraham Zapruder, a film that only three members of the Warren Commission had seen, probably because it cast a long shadow of doubt across their conclusions. A good analysis of the film can be found in *Cover-Up* by J. Gary Shaw and Larry Harris:

> Had the Zapruder film of the JFK assassination been shown on national television Friday evening, November 22, 1963, the Oswald/lone assassin fabrication would have been unacceptable to a majority of Americans. . . . The car proceeds down Elm and briefly disappears behind a sign. When it

emerges the President has obviously been shot. . . . Gov.
Connally turns completely to the right, looking into the
back seat; he begins to turn back when his body stiffens on
impact of a bullet. Very shortly after Connally is hit, the
President's head explodes in a shower of blood and brain
matter—he is driven violently backward at a speed estimated at 80–100 feet per second.

Although Time, Inc. could have made a small fortune dis-
tributing this film around the world, they instead secured the
rights from Zapruder for $225,000, then held a few private
screenings before locking the film in a vault. It was shown to
one newsman, Dan Rather, who then described it on national
television. Rather asserted that Kennedy's head went "forward
with considerable force" after the fatal head shot (a statement
that would have supported a hit from behind, from the direc-
tion of the School Book Depository). Several months later,
Rather was promoted to White House Correspondent by CBS.
As if to buttress this fabrication, the FBI reversed the order of
the frames when printing them in the Warren Report. When
researchers later drew this reversal to the FBI's attention,
Hoover attributed the switch to a "printing error."

Although Garrison proved his conspiracy, the jury was not
convinced of Clay Shaw's role in it. He was released after only
two hours of deliberation.

6

The CIA Did Not Plot to Kill John F. Kennedy

Massimo Polidoro

Massimo Polidoro is executive director of the Italian Committee for the Investigation of Claims of the Paranormal and has investigated dozens of cases of supposed paranormal events. The results of Polidoro's work have been published in both the Skeptical Inquirer *magazine and the* Journal of the Society for Psychical Research.

Conspiracy theories concerning the assassination of President John F. Kennedy have been widely disseminated for over forty years. Those who have put forth theories in books, films, and on Web sites have often relied on eyewitness accounts of the event. However, as any defense attorney will argue, eyewitness testimony is notoriously inaccurate. Fearful people caught in the midst of a crime will often imagine events that never really happened. In the Kennedy case, one eyewitness, Jean Hill, has made something of a career out of being in close proximity to the president when he was murdered. However, Hill's recollections are fraught with inaccuracies that can easily be disproved. With this in mind, those constructing elaborate conspiracy theories concerning Kennedy should be cautious about relying on statements from witnesses. In addition, investigators of historical mysteries need to be wary of self-styled experts who make claims that will eventually be refuted by real experts. The available evidence shows that Kennedy was killed by one bullet shot by Lee Harvey Oswald.

Hundreds of books and thousands of articles have been written about the tragic death of President John Fitzgerald Kennedy, and it would take a few complete issues of *Skeptical Inquirer* just to deal with the more relevant matters involved in the case. I will outline several examples of bad research involved in popular investigations of this case.

Let's get back to that fatal day, November 22, 1963. President Kennedy arrived in Dallas, Texas, during the election campaign. In 1964, there would have been new elections, and Kennedy, who wanted to be sure to be re-elected, had started a tour of the southern states, the most conservative ones, where he was less popular due to his progressive ideas.

It was decided that a motorcade would be conducted through the city. Kennedy and his wife would be in the backseat of the presidential limousine, and Governor Connally and his wife would sit in front of them.

Dealey Plaza, in downtown Dallas, is a large, basin-like square where three roads converge toward an underpass that leads to a freeway. The Presidential limousine entered the plaza, moved slowly along Houston Street, then took a left turn right in front of the Texas School Book Depository building.

It was soon determined that the shots came from the sixth floor of the Book Depository.

It was thirty minutes past noon. What happened next was documented by a movie buff, Abraham Zapruder, who was filming the motorcade with an 8 mm movie camera. The film is silent, for there was no audio on home-movie cameras back then. During the shocking sequence, the President can be seen waving to the crowd, but then he is hit by something and brings his hands to his neck, right in front of him. Governor

Connally starts to turn and shake, he is hit as well. Then, there is a fatal shot to Kennedy's head. He died soon after at the hospital.

Who killed him? It was soon determined that the shots came from the sixth floor of the Book Depository. There, piles of boxes were found, stashed around a window, creating a "sniper's nest" with a clear view of the site of the shooting. A rifle was also found that had just been fired along with three spent cartridge shells.

After about two hours, a suspect was stopped. He had had a confrontation with the police inside a movie theater, and it was later found out that he had just shot dead a policeman who had stopped him on a nearby street.

His name was Lee Harvey Oswald; he was a young man who worked at the depository and had been seen on the sixth floor of that building just minutes before the shooting. After that, he disappeared, and he turned out to be the only employee absent from the depository for no legitimate reason.

Oswald was an ex-marine and communist sympathizer. The evidence against him quickly piled up, but only three days after his capture, during his transfer to a police van that would escort him to a more secure prison, nightclub owner Jack Ruby shot him dead.

A Conspiracy Unravels

Those of you who have seen the Oliver Stone movie *JFK,* where this story is told in great detail, will remember the many contradictions coming out of the official investigation of the assassination. I have seen that movie as well, and, like anyone else, I couldn't help but be convinced that Oswald could not be the only assassin. There had to be more than one killer, and this meant that there had been a conspiracy plot to kill the president.

At least, I believed that until I started to research the story for my latest book, and the strangest thing to me was that the deeper I went into it, the more the Oliver Stone version of the story looked weirder and weirder.

I can't go into the countless details here, as I have done in the book, but I'll give you just a couple of examples of the kind of pitfalls into which a historical investigator can easily fall.

I Saw It; I Was There . . .

Most strange phenomena and conspiracy theories rely on eye-witness testimony. Psychologists are aware of the many limits of memory and perception—and the fallibility of eyewitness accounts.

One of the best-known witnesses to the assassination, and the only one who is also the author of a book from the point of view of an eyewitness, was a woman named Jean Hill. She can be seen in the Zapruder film, standing beside a friend.

Oswald was an ex-marine and communist sympathizer. The evidence against him quickly piled up.

In her testimony, told and retold over the last forty years, she claimed among other things that she was looking at the limousine where she saw Kennedy and his wife, Jackie; the couple was "looking at a little dog between them," a "white fluffy dog." Hill then jumped to the edge of the street to yell, "Hey, we want to take your picture!" JFK turned over to look at her. At that point, he was shot, and Jackie shouted, "My God, he has been shot!" Then, Mrs. Hill said that she saw "some men in plain clothes shooting back" and "a man with a hat running toward the monument" on the other side of the plaza on the so-called "grassy knoll." Immediately, she started running after him, thinking he was involved in the shooting. "When I ran across the street," she specified, "the first motor-cycle that was right behind the President's car nearly hit me."

Thus, she was the first person to run up the grassy knoll, and many followed her. However, the man ran off and she missed him. She was convinced that this man was Jack Ruby, the club owner who, in three days, would kill Lee Harvey Oswald.

And there we have our proof for the existence of a conspiracy.

Psychologists are aware of the many limits of memory and perception—and the fallibility of eyewitness accounts.

This, however, is one of those rare occasions in which dozens of reporters and photographers are present on the scene of an event and so there are countless statements on record from eyewitnesses and pictures from every angle. Thus, we can compare Jean Hill's memory with actual facts.

- She said that she was looking at the limousine.

In the film, you can see that when Kennedy is shot the first time, she is looking away from him.

- She said that the couple was "looking at a little dog between them," a "white fluffy dog."

There was no dog between them, just a bunch of red flowers.

- She said that she "jumped to the edge of the street" to yell, "Hey, we want to take your picture!" and JFK turned over to look at her.

The Zapruder film shows that Hill never moved or said a word—and the President did not turn to look over. In fact, he had just been shot when he passed in front of her.

- She said that Jackie shouted, "My God, he has been shot!"

> *Jackie and the car's four other witnesses deny that Jackie said anything.*

- She said that she saw "some men in plain clothes shooting back."

> *But in an interview recorded just forty minutes after the assassination by a Dallas television station, she was asked: "Did you see the person who fired the—" And she answered: "No . . . I didn't see any person fire the weapon . . . I only heard it."*

- She said that she immediately started running after the "man with a hat," thinking he was involved in the shooting. "When I ran across the street," she specified, "the first motorcycle that was right behind the President's car nearly hit me."

> *But as can be seen in the many pictures taken during those fatal moments, she stands still at her place as the limousine and the motorbikes pass by. She even sits on the grass while all of the cars of the motorcade proceed behind the President's limousine.*

- She also specified that after jumping into the middle of the road, she was the first person to run up the grassy knoll, and many followed her.

> *In photographs, you can see a lot of people running around the area and up to the grassy knoll, but Hill always stays in the same spot, probably shocked by the whole thing, like most of the people present.*

- She was convinced that the man she had followed was Jack Ruby.

> *At that precise moment, Ruby was witnessed by many to be at the offices of the* Dallas Morning News.

Now, as we can see, facts contradict many details of Jean Hill's dramatic testimony. Aside from excusable mistakes and errors made in good faith, we have here a story that, over the years, has changed and grown out of proportion, to the point that Mrs. Hill became a sort of celebrity, invited to every meeting of JFK buffs, and was even depicted in Oliver Stone's movie. She is the proud holder of a card bragging that she was the "closest witness" to the President at the time of the fatal shot to the head. It is quite clear what happens to some people when they find themselves right in the middle of history and have absolutely no role in it. They imagine one.

This Must Be So; I Know . . .

Imagined testimonies are just one of the many problems that an investigator of historical mysteries has to deal with. Another one is "imagined experts," that is, self-styled experts with no real expertise in the chosen field except what they think is "common sense." The Kennedy assassination presents dozens of such cases, but one of the most popular involves the so-called "magic bullet."

The Warren Commission that investigated the Kennedy assassination concluded that the reactions of Kennedy and Connally occurred too close together for two separate shots, even from the same gun, to have been responsible for their wounds. They almost seem to react at the same instant, in the enhanced version of the film seen by the commission. They concluded that one, single bullet caused the injuries to both the President and the Governor.

Before you know it, you start twisting facts and discarding evidence that contradict those ideas, making you draw unfounded solutions.

This is where the "imagined experts" step in and say: "It must have been a really magical bullet in order to enter Kennedy from the back, exit from his throat, then make a turn and enter Connally's back, exit from his chest, hit his right wrist, make another bend, and, finally, land in his left thigh!" How could a single bullet follow this zigzag route?

Their conclusion is obvious: those injuries could not have been produced by just one bullet, so there had to be more than one shooter—further proof of a conspiracy.

This conclusion, however, as logical as it may sound at first, does not take real facts into account. And it only works until you don't look at Kennedy's and Connally's actual positions in the car. They were not one in front of the other; Kennedy was in a higher position in the back seat, and Connally was sitting lower, in the middle of the front seat of the car. So, in order to produce those injuries . . . from the analysis performed by real experts, it turns out that there was only one position from which this bullet could be shot: the sixth floor of the Texas School Book Depository.

What can we conclude from these examples? Certainly, that investigators must guard against preconceived ideas before starting an investigation. Before you know it, you start twisting facts and discarding evidence that contradict those ideas, making you draw unfounded solutions. What we should do instead is to try to do our best to dig up facts and let them speak for themselves. They may have things to say that often turn out to be quite surprising.

7

The Government Is Hiding the Discovery of UFOs

Steven M. Greer

Steven M. Greer is an emergency-room physician and the founder and director of the Disclosure Project. This organization was formed to record and publicize the testimony of military, government, and other witnesses who have seen UFOs.

Contrary to assertions by the government and military officials, UFOs have already landed on Earth. However, authorities are keeping the information about the extraterrestrial visitors secret in order to carry out a monumental conspiracy to take control of the planet through the use of the aliens' technology. In order to instigate this plot, a shadowy government group, big business, and the media have been creating a fear of aliens in the American public by spreading false stories about cattle mutilations and abductions reportedly carried out by extraterrestrials. Next, the conspirators will stage a horrific attack on Earth and make it appear as though aliens are responsible for it. This hoax will allow them to manipulate the public, who will presumably sacrifice their democratic freedoms in exchange for protection from alleged alien attacks. This conspiracy to initiate an era of total war in space must be stopped by those who value freedom and peace over war and cosmic insanity.

Imagine this. It is the summer of 2001, and someone presents you with a script for a movie or book that tells how a diabolical terrorist plot unfolds wherein both 110 story World

Trade Center towers and part of the Pentagon are destroyed by commercial jets hijacked and flown into those structures.

Of course you would laugh, and if you were a movie mogul or book editor, reject it out of hand as ridiculous and implausible, even for a fictional novel or movie. After all, how could a commercial jet, being tracked on radar after two jets had already hit the World Trade towers, make it through our air defenses, into the most sensitive airspace in the world, and in broad daylight on a crystal clear day, slam into the Pentagon! And this in a country that spends over $1 billion a day to defend itself! Absurd, illogical—nobody would swallow it!

Unfortunately, there are some of us who have seen these scripts—and of far worse things to come—and we are not laughing.

One of the few silver linings to these recent tragedies is that maybe—just maybe—people will take seriously, however far-fetched it may seem at first, the prospect that a shadowy, para-governmental and transnational entity exists that has kept UFOs secret—and is planning a deception and tragedy that will dwarf the events of 9/11.

The testimony of hundreds of government, military and corporate insiders has established this: That UFOs are real, that some are built by our secret 'black' shadowy government projects and some are from extraterrestrial civilizations, and that a group has kept this secret so that the technology behind the UFO can be withheld—until the right time. This technology can—and eventually will—replace the need for oil, gas, coal, ionizing nuclear power, and other centralized and highly destructive energy systems.

This 5 trillion dollar industry—energy and transportation—is currently highly centralized, metered and lucrative. It is the stuff that runs the entire industrialized world. It is the mother of all special interests. It is not about money as you and I think of it, but about geopolitical power—the very centralized power on which the current order in the world runs.

The world is kept in a state of rolling wars, endless poverty for most of Earth's denizens and global environmental ruin, just to prop up this evil world order.

Control Through Fear

As immense as that game is, there is a bigger one: Control through fear. As [rocket scientist] Wernher von Braun related to Dr. Carol Rosin, his spokesperson for the last 4 years of his life, a maniacal machine—the military, industrial, intelligence, laboratory complex—would go from Cold War, to Rogue Nations, to Global Terrorism (the stage we find ourselves at today), to the ultimate trump card: A hoaxed threat from space.

To justify eventually spending trillions of dollars on space weapons, the world would be deceived about a threat from outer space, thus uniting the world in fear, in militarism, and in war.

A shadowy, para-governmental and transnational entity exists that has kept UFOs secret—and is planning a deception and tragedy that will dwarf the events of 9/11.

Since 1992 I have seen this script unveiled to me by at least a dozen well-placed insiders. Of course, initially I laughed, thinking this just too absurd and far-fetched. Dr. Rosin gave her testimony to the Disclosure Project before 9/11. And yet others told me explicitly that things that looked like UFOs but that are built and under the control of deeply secretive 'black' projects, were being used to simulate—hoax—ET-appearing events, including some abductions and cattle mutilations, to sow the early seeds of cultural fear regarding life in outer space. And that at some point after global terrorism, events would unfold that would utilize the now-revealed Alien Reproduction Vehicles (ARVs, or reversed-engineered UFOs made by humans by studying actual ET craft) to hoax an attack on Earth.

Like the movie "Independence Day", an attempt to unite the world through militarism would unfold using ET as the new cosmic scapegoat (think Jews during the Third Reich).

None of this is new to me or other insiders. The report from Iron Mountain, NY, written in the 1960s, described the need to demonize life in outer space so we could have a new enemy. An enemy off-planet that could unite humans (in fear and war) and that would prove to be the ultimate prop for the trillion dollar military industrial complex that conservative Republican President and five star general [Dwight D.] Eisenhower warned us about in 1961 (no one was listening then, either. . .).

The Post-9/11 Script

So here is the post-9/11 script—one that will be played out unless enough people are informed and the plan can be foiled because they will be unable to fool a sufficient number of citizens and leaders:

After a period of terrorism—a period during which the detonation of nuclear devices will be threatened and possibly actuated, thus justifying expanding the weaponization of space—an effort will ramp up to present the public with information about a threat from outer space. Not just asteroids hitting the Earth, but other threats. An extraterrestrial threat.

Over the past 40 years, UFOlogy, as it is called, combined with a mighty media machine, has increasingly demonized ETs via fearsome movies like "Independence Day", and pseudo-science that presents alien kidnappings and abuse as a fact (in some circles) of modern life. That some humans have had contact with ETs I have no doubt; that the real ET contact has been subsumed in an ocean of hoaxed accounts I am certain.

That is, real ET events are seldom reported out to the public. The Machine ensures that the hoaxed, frightening and intrinsically xenophobic accounts are the ones seen and read by millions. This mental conditioning to fear ET has been subtly reinforced for decades, in preparation for future deceptions. Deceptions that will make 9/11 look trivial.

I write this now because I have recently been contacted by several highly placed media and intelligence sources that have made it clear to me that hoaxed events and story-lines are imminent that will attempt to further ramp up the fear machine regarding UFOs and ETs. After all, to have an enemy, you must make the people hate and fear a person, a group of people, or in this case an entire category of beings.

To be clear: the maniacal covert programs controlling UFO secrecy, ARVs and related technologies—including those technologies that can simulate ET events, ET abductions and the like—plan to hijack Disclosure, spin it into the fire of fear, and roll out events that will eventually present ETs as a new enemy. Do not be deceived.

Hoaxed events and story-lines are imminent that will attempt to further ramp up the fear machine regarding UFOs and ETs.

This hogwash, already the stuff of countless books, videos, movies, documentaries and the like, will attempt to glom onto the facts, evidence and first-hand insider testimony of The Disclosure Project, and on its coattails, deliver to the world the cosmic deception that falsely portrays ETs as a threat from space. Do not be deceived.

Pretext for a War in Space

By commingling fact with fiction, and by hoaxing UFO events that can look terrifying, the Plan is to eventually create a new, sustainable, off-planet enemy. And who will be the wiser?

You will. Because now you know that after 60 years, trillions of dollars and the best scientific minds in the world pressed into action, a secretive, shadowy group—a government within the government and at once fully outside the government as we know it—has mastered the technologies, the art of deception, and the capability to launch an attack on Earth and make it look like ETs did it. In 1997, I brought a man to Washington to brief members of Congress and others about this plan. Our entire team at the time met this man. He had been present at planning sessions when ARVs—things built by Lockheed, Northrup, et al., and housed in secretive locations around the world—would be used to simulate an attack on certain assets, making leaders and citizens alike believe that there was a threat from space, when there is none. (Before he could testify, his handlers spirited him away to a secret location in Virginia until the briefing was over....) Sound familiar? Wernher von Braun warned of such a hoax, as a pretext for putting war in space. And many others have warned of the same.

A government within the government ... has mastered the technologies, the art of deception, and the capability to launch an attack on Earth and make it look like ETs did it.

Space based weapons are already in place—part of a secret parallel space program that has been operating since the 1960s. ARVs are built and ready to go (see the book *Disclosure* and the chapter with the testimony of Mark McCandlish et al.). Space holographic deception technologies are in place, tested and ready to fire. And the Big Media is a pawn, now taking dictation from the right hand of the king.

I know this all sounds like science fiction. Absurd. Impossible. Just like 9/11 would have sounded before 9/11. But the unthinkable happened and may happen again, unless we are vigilant.

Combine all of this with the current atmosphere of fear and manipulation and there is a real risk of suspending our collective judgment and our constitution.

But know this: If there was a threat from outer space, we would have known about it as soon as humans started exploding nuclear weapons and going into space with manned travel. That we are still breathing the free air of Earth, given the galacticly stupid and reckless actions of an out of control, illegal, secret group, is abundant testimony to the restraint and peaceful intentions of these visitors. The threat is wholly human. And it is we who must address this threat, rein it in and transform the current situation of war, destruction and secret manipulation to one of true Disclosure and an era of sustained peace.

War in space, to replace war on Earth, is not evolution, but cosmic madness. A world thus united in fear is worse than one divided by ignorance. It is now time for the great leap into the future, a leap that moves us out of fear and ignorance and into an unbroken era of universal peace. Know that this is our destiny. And it will be ours just as soon as we choose it.

8

The Government Did Not Cover Up UFO Visits

B.D. Gildenberg

B.D. Gildenberg spent thirty-five years working with the top secret government aerospace program Skyhook. He has authored or coauthored many magazine articles that disprove UFO theories while revealing details of Skyhook.

Beginning in 1947 the U.S. government carried out hundreds of top secret military missions using giant balloons that were often mistaken for UFOs. Under the classified Skyhook program, these huge floating objects were used to spy on the former Soviet Union nuclear program, study atmospheric landing conditions for launching missiles, and gather data for the Apollo moon landing project. After nearly every launch of a Skyhook project, local authorities received reports of UFO sightings. While the government was aware of this problem, Skyhook was so secret that even local police could not be notified of its existence. Now that the Soviet Union has collapsed and Skyhook and other Cold War programs have been discontinued, their details are being declassified. Although some people continue to believe that the government was involved in a conspiracy to hide the existence of UFOs, its real secret was its Cold War activities.

I was busy calibrating instrumentation for top-secret Project Mogul in the spring of 1947. In retrospect, I was totally unaware of the project's actual identity. My security clearance

B.D. Gildenberg, "The Cold War's Classified Skyhook Program," *The Skeptical Inquirer,* May 2004. Copyright © 2004 by the Committee for the Scientific Investigation of Claims of the Paranormal. Reproduced by permission.

was for the lower rating of confidential. I was unaware of the project title for another forty-eight years, until 1995.

Welcome to the arcane world of classified Skyhook programs and Cold War intrigue. In this review, I hope to reveal many of those once-classified programs, how they generated UFO mythology, and why that relationship has not been fully addressed.

I write from a thirty-five-year professional career as a Skyhook balloon specialist and direct experience with most of the programs in these revelations. I was also an investigator for a special Project Blue Office and years later worked on the Pentagon Roswell report.

A Skyhook balloon provides constant-level performance at a predetermined altitude. It is usually constructed of special plastics and can lift tons of payload for durations of days or longer. The latter capability was once highly classified. Skyhook balloons were huge. The average size of those discussed in this article was double the six million cubic feet of the *Hindenburg* [the German zeppelin whose fiery crash in New Jersey in 1937 made international headlines]. Their diameters were about 300 feet with a flaccid length of 430 feet. Primarily cruising in the stratosphere, the balloons change color at high altitudes during sunrises and sunsets, while the Earth below is almost dark. These characteristics equate to a superb UFO generator.

It is therefore more than a coincidence that the birth of this vehicle in 1947 coincided with the origin of the twentieth century UFO epidemic. That epidemic was highlighted by the Roswell incident, with Project Mogul the prime seed. . . .

The Skyhook Program

The prime launch site for Project Mogul was Alamogordo Air Base in New Mexico, west and therefore upwind of Roswell. The 1947 launches were in June and July, but there were initial UFO reports around the East Coast prior to the summer.

These were preliminary test launches from New Jersey and Long Island.

There were also sightings in the summer of 1947 in the western and northwestern United States. A 1949 Air Force investigation could not correlate those sightings with Project Mogul, but the Air Force was unaware of a Navy program launching cluster balloons in Colorado that same summer. Coordination between branches of the military was limited in the years just following World War II. Accordingly, the dilemma of that 1949 report added fuel to a developing UFO mythology.

The balloons change color at high altitudes during sunrises and sunsets, while the Earth below is almost dark. These characteristics equate to a superb UFO generator.

Clusters of weather balloons launched from both New Mexico and Colorado triggered reports of flying saucers sighted in formations throughout the West. They briefly preceded plastic Skyhook balloons, but their performance as constant-level vehicles was marginal.

An initial government cover-up for Project Mogul saw an assembled crew not associated with the project launching a similar configuration, but without the classified payload. Newspapers were invited to the launch again at Alamogordo Air Base. Years later, as the Roswell legend resurfaced, UFO proponents denounced Project Mogul as a cover-up for their alien event.

At Alamogordo AFB [Air Force Base] headquarters, Mogul was listed as a guided-missile program. That represented a further cover-up procedure. The actual purpose of the project was stratospheric detection of distant nuclear bomb tests. Unknown to Roswell enthusiasts were classified programs that operated for decades afterward, based on Project Mogul technology.

One unclassified derivative was Project Blue Book, the Air Force investigation of UFOs. An initial sponsor was the Air Material Command, headquarters for Project Mogul. Blue Book originated in January, 1948, under the title Project Sign. Project Mogul prompted the initial development of a USAF [U.S. Air Force] Skyhook facility at Alamogordo AFB (today Holloman AFB). It was eventually governed by the Cambridge Research Laboratories in Massachusetts and became the prime USAF Skyhook launch site, still active today. Project Blue Book had outlying reporting offices throughout the country. Their function was to gather UFO reports and send them to the Blue Book main office at Wright Field, Ohio.

At Holloman AFB, the Blue Book office was situated in our Skyhook Balloon building. That choice was biased by the significant percent of reports generated by our relatively new vehicle. This office was also unique in that it, like the Wright Field Center, analyzed reports. I joined the Holloman Skyhook group in 1951 for a thirty-year tour and immediately became involved with Project Blue Book.

There was a more discrete reason for this special Blue Book role. In 1951, we became the primary center for unclassified Project Moby Dick. In at least one pro-Roswell book that project was erroneously dated 1947 and classified as secret. Such misinformation contributes to the mythology of government cover-ups.

Rumors and Cover-Ups

Project Moby Dick's stated purpose was to study stratosphere wind trajectories, as defined via three-day Skyhook flights. After training for over a year at our location, crews and equipment moved to three West Coast sites for the operational phase. Although the announced purpose did result in final reports containing those stratospheric trajectories, there was actually a secretive phase. Moby Dick was in fact a cover-up for top-secret project WS-119L.

Besides the alphanumeric title, secret projects have secret names that vary for different phases. This program was called Project Gopher at our Alamogordo AFB launch site. It later accumulated titles including Grayback, Moby Dick Hi, Gentrix, and Grandson.

Even the WS prefix was a cover-up, since it was not a weapon system. The actual project goal was balloon reconnaissance of the Soviet Union. . . . Project Moby Dick was actually gathering trajectory data for Project Gopher, although the information also generated unclassified data for meteorological applications.

We flew five Gopher (WS-119L) test flights in 1951 and 1952 from our Air Force Skyhook Center. The payload was kept in a hanger during flight preparation under continuous armed guard. Outsiders noticed this and ensuing rumors eventually generated tales including a secret Project Aquarius. . . . The mythology of Project Aquarius is nebulous but has something to do with an MJ-12[1] committee maintaining communications with Roswell aliens.

All this intrigue came to a head when the CIA suddenly showed up at our office and at launches. UFO reports peaked in 1952, as our local Skyhook activity increased from ninety-two hours the previous year to 694 hours aloft. Moreover, launches from the Moby Dick West Coast sites were commencing. Eventually they, along with additional sites in Missouri and Georgia, contributed 640 flights.

Clusters of weather balloons launched from both New Mexico and Colorado triggered reports of flying saucers sighted in formations throughout the West.

The CIA requested that we not identify most of those sharply increasing Skyhook reports. The strategy was to generate a UFO outbreak over the USA extending to the USSR

1. Majestic 12, an alleged secret government committee formed to investigate UFOs

when our WS-119L Skyhooks arrived there. Ironically, the ploy initially worked, since the Soviet Air Force could not intercept the first wave. They allowed their public to play our UFO game. The strategy ended after a few leaking Skyhooks were shot down and the payloads were exhibited, along with protests, to President Eisenhower.

Thus, complex interplay of Moby Dick, WS-119L, and UFO reports defined the unique role of our Blue Book office in that era. Since top-secret WS-119L was not declassified until more than thirty years later, that intrigue can only now be addressed. . . .

The entire Skyhook reconnaissance program produced marginal data, but its recovery techniques phased into satellite programs. Moreover, the Soviets were so impressed they actually developed several high-altitude aircraft dedicated to intercepting our Skyhooks! In the 1960s, [Soviet] Premier [Nikita] Khrushchev developed a habit of banging his shoe on the table in protest at the UN. In one such case, he exhibited a WS-119L payload, perhaps with some of our trainees' initials on it.

Late in 1952, I spent a month at Edwards AFB, California, to forecast three-day trajectories for Moby Dick flights, as specified in my travel orders. Forty years later, I discovered from [historian Curtis] Peebles's *The Moby Dick Project* that I actually had been working on a top-secret program called Flying Cloud, WS-124A!

Skyhooks were to be evaluated as a balloon bomber in the event of an actual war. Proposed payloads included nuclear warheads, but the program was abandoned as intercontinental ballistic missiles became viable.

UFO Mythology

There were a number of peripheral events associated with these programs. At Alamogordo AFB in 1952, we dispatched F-86 jet aircraft to see if they could intercept our Skyhooks at various altitudes. The exercise was designed to evaluate what Soviet interceptors might experience when our reconnaissance balloons arrived. The event was described in Timothy Good's *Above Top Secret* published thirty-six years later. It represents a classic example of how portrayals of classified military testing can become transformed over decades into something out of this world. Date and aircraft type were correct but the latter were described as trying to intercept an evasive UFO that featured hovering and accelerations up to 700 mph.

Alamogordo Air Force Base was renamed Holloman AFB in 1953. On October 27 of that year, we launched an unclassified payload. It failed to terminate at the scheduled twelve-hour flight duration, and, six days later, it was detected by the Royal Air Force over the Atlantic headed for London! This of course generated UFO hysteria. Newspapers announced it could not be a Skyhook since there was presently no such activity in Europe, but altitude and performance reports agreed with our vehicle's capabilities. Ironically, British intelligence officers also knew that but would not disclose the object's identity. They too were involved with the WS-119L program, and test flights were to be launched from Scotland. Yet this incident is still highlighted in UFO literature as a classic case for their cause.

We flew a few classified programs in the late 1950s and 1960s which included special flares at night from twenty-mile altitudes. That was a predictable UFO generator.

[Project] Grab Bag generated probably the most detailed UFO events in the literature.

Philip Corso's book *The Day After Roswell* contained many significant errors including movements of some of [rocket scientist] Wernher von Braun's German scientists, who shared our building at Holloman AFB. Sixty pages were dedicated to a once-secret U.S. Army project for a lunar base called Project

Horizon. Plans were initiated in 1959 but were finally cancelled because Project Apollo had exhausted space funds. The story was suspiciously infused with hints of alien activity on the Moon. That was interesting because that same year my Skyhook Center was flying a classified Army project, code named ... Project Horizon! It had nothing to do with lunar bases and involved photographic studies of the horizon. The purpose was to obtain calibration information for guided missiles.

Proceedings were so classified that they could not identify their mission under any circumstance.

In 1967 and 1969, we flew ever more advanced, classified reconnaissance cameras. These cameras were huge, weighing from 6,000 to 8,000 pounds, and encased in ten-foot cylinders. They were tracked by several helicopters carrying armed military police to surround the payload after landing. With Roswell often downwind, this very likely contributed to that UFO story line, and time compaction is a vital ingredient in creating such myths and legends.

Project Grab Bag

Skyhook incidents near to or on the ground, like this previous case, provoked more UFO tales than balloons at an altitude. There was a cluster of this type of event in the 1960s, which evoked much media coverage. It persists today as a hallmark UFO case, and features the most detailed witness descriptions.

One of those events had serious overtones, involving sensitive military sites, with no obvious revelations to this date. It is noted in Good's book, *Above Top Secret*. "A metallic disc-shaped UFO with bright flashing lights moving slowly over the site. It stopped and hovered at 500 feet then the UFO climbed vertically and disappeared at high speed" (this was in March, 1967). The location was a Minuteman missile site at

Minor, North Dakota. I became suspicious after reading this, aware of a top-secret Skyhook program in that era, with one launch site in the Dakotas. There were other descriptions that rather precisely identified the program, despite scattered inclusions of media mythology.

The program was Project Grab Bag, also called Sky Dipper or Cold Ash. Again, there was a cover-up unclassified program, Program Ash Can. Both programs involved sampling radioactive fallout debris in the stratosphere. After a brief Navy test sequence, Grab Bag, now under the USAF, became operational in 1956, extending briefly into the 1970s. Its highly classified signature was due to the fact that a final product involved establishing details of Soviet plutonium production. Even our Project Ash Can attracted more than the usual Skyhook attention, since parachute and payload were snatched in midair by USAF cargo aircraft. That prompted stories of aircraft being attacked by a UFO while the mother ship (the Skyhook) hovered high above.

Clearly, secret Skyhook balloon programs magnified government cover-ups and engendered numerous UFO stories, sightings, and myths.

Grab Bag was a special UFO generator. After stratospheric sampling, lifting gas was partially released through a valve in the apex of the Skyhook. The entire ensemble was thus lowered to within a few thousand feet of the ground. Then it released a parachute with the payload while the under-loaded balloon rocketed upward to eventually shatter. Since most of these activities occurred at night, Grab Bag generated probably the most detailed UFO events in the literature. For instance, "A conical shaped object descended from the sky. It hovered at an estimated 3,000 feet. A smaller UFO landed within fifty feet."

That is a precise description of the basic Grab Bag profile. The Minuteman case with a UFO climbing vertically to disappear at high speed sounds very much like the under- loaded balloon zooming skyward to disappear as it self-destructed.

Project tracking included three helicopters. If the winds were light, the entire ensemble would be valved to the surface. Again, UFO reports clearly identified the process. "Floating red lights which moved over a highway and into a field at night. It appeared like a two-story building, with other lights grouped around it. The latter sometimes hover around the central object."

The payload did indeed have red lights. The other hovering lights were the helicopters. Just before landing the sample would be transferred to another container via a powerful centrifugal blower. That noise amplified the mystery. Occasionally the tracking crew would transfer the sample into metal cylinders, engendering even more strange noises in the dark. Other activity was also reported: "Radiation fields and other forms of energy have appeared to be directly connected with a hovering or landed UFO." The radioactivity, although slight, was from the sample being transferred by recovery personnel to another container.

Ghost Copters Buzzing Ranches

Readers may wonder why, after recovery, Grab Bag personnel would not have notified local authorities without disclosing classification. The answer is that proceedings were so classified that they could not identify their mission under any circumstance. The program was a natural for engendering mystery and a treasury of lucrative narratives for UFO folklore. Meanwhile, at our Holloman AFB Skyhook Center, we continued to launch a variety of classified reconnaissance cameras, now with loads up to five tons. Again, there were tracking helicopters with armed military police (MPs). People in southern New Mexico were used to seeing military helicopters on various missions. However, we flew a number of reconnaissance camera missions in 1975 in northeastern New Mexico where military helicopters were seldom seen. This created some suspicion. "Unidentified helicopters" had also helped to amplify Grab Bag as a UFO generator, triggering later myths involving military helicopters.

There was an outbreak of mutilated cattle stories in Colorado and northeastern New Mexico in 1975. Strange helicopters were part of the scenario. The *Albuquerque Journal* reported "ghost copters" buzzing ranches. The presence of armed MPs onboard added to the frenzy. The FAA [Federal Aviation Administration] Area Coordinator announced an investigation of this outbreak but never revealed what it had found. The FBI also became involved with similar results. Both agencies had quickly discovered it was our highly classified program. Their "case closed" reaction is still highlighted today in government cover-up tales.

Many Pentagon authorities believed that the Roswell and UFO investigations in general were not worthy of distraction from more pressing matters of national importance.

Clearly, secret Skyhook balloon programs magnified government cover-ups and engendered numerous UFO stories, sightings, and myths. Classified aircraft also contributed to UFO folklore during the Cold War. The U-2 reconnaissance aircraft followed WS-119L operations over the USSR. It triggered similar UFO reports, even while training in the U.S. However, unlike supersonic aircraft, Skyhooks remained within sight for long durations, landing with strange payloads, far from their origin.

It is important that all this activity be revealed. Project Grab Bag generated the most detailed descriptions of UFOs in the literature. Even relatively skeptical individuals might have wondered about those sightings, believing them to be too complex to dismiss. I hope these revelations provide a vital insight into what was "behind the looking glass" of secret Cold War activities.

The Pentagon published the first two detailed reports in 1995, demonstrating how top-secret Project Mogul became the initial trigger for the Roswell mystery. Readers may wonder why that effort has not been repeated for once-classified events detailed in this article. Actually, it was only at the urging of a congressman, the late Steve Schiff of New Mexico, that the Pentagon began work on the Roswell affair. Having participated in the preparation of the final report, I can reveal there was substantial resistance to the whole process. A number of times we thought the enterprise would be cancelled. It was only via last-minute intervention by the Secretary of the Air Force that the report was finally published. Many Pentagon authorities believed that the Roswell and UFO investigations in general were not worthy of distraction from more pressing matters of national importance.

Despite providing accurate hardware descriptions of the programs we have covered, some reports included stories of onboard aliens and other typical elements of UFO mythology such as stalled cars and skin burns. They were imitating numerous UFO witnesses with a tendency to repeat stories that preceded their own sightings.

Organizations to Contact

Above Top Secret (ATS)
Web site: www.abovetopsecret.com

Above Top Secret is a global community of about forty thousand people who share a sense of urgency about current events and their effects on the future of mankind. ATS attempts to expose conspiracies perpetrated by the government, businesses, and the media. The organization publishes blogs and the weekly *ATS Newsletter,* available by e-mail.

Central Intelligence Agency (CIA)
Office of Public Affairs, Washington, DC 20505
(703) 482-0623 • fax: (703) 482-1739
Web site: www.cia.gov

The CIA was created in 1947 with the signing of the National Security Act (NSA) by President Harry S. Truman. The NSA charged the director of the CIA with coordinating the nation's intelligence activities and correlating, evaluating, and disseminating intelligence that affects national security. Publications, including *Factbook on Intelligence* and *The CIA in the New World Order: Intelligence Challenges Through 2015,* are available on its Web site.

Committee for the Scientific Investigation of Claims of the Paranormal
PO Box 703, Amherst, NY 14226
(716) 636-1425
e-mail: info@csicop.org
Web site: www.csicop.org

The Committee for the Scientific Investigation of Claims of the Paranormal encourages critical investigation into claims of paranormal events and conspiracy theories from a scientific point of view. The group disseminates information about the results of such inquiries to the scientific community and the general public through its Web site, its quarterly newsletter *Skeptical Briefs,* and its magazine *Skeptical Inquirer.*

The Disclosure Project
PO Box 4556, Largo, MD 20775
(301) 249-3915 • fax: (501) 325-8328
e-mail: media@disclosureproject.org
Web site: www.disclosureproject.org

The goal of the Disclosure Project is to hold open congressional hearings on the existence of UFO and extraterrestrials (ETs) on and around Earth. The hearings would rely on testimony from scores of military, government, and other witnesses who have seen UFOs and ETs. The Disclosure Project also claims that ETs have created advanced energy and propulsion systems that can provide solutions to global environmental challenges. The organization publishes books such as *Extraterrestrial Contact,* and videotapes and audiotapes featuring interviews with those who claim to have made contact with aliens from outer space.

Freemasons
Masonic Information Center, 81200 Fenton St.
  Silver Spring, MD 20910-4785
(301) 588-4010 • fax: (301) 608-3457
e-mail: msana@ix.netcom.com
Web site: www.rsm-mi.org/facts.html

The 2 million Masons (also known as Freemasons) belong to the oldest and largest fraternal organization in the world. The organization uses the tools and implements of ancient architectural craftsmen symbolically in a system of instruction designed to build character and moral values in its members. Masonry teaches that each person, through self-improvement and helping others, has an obligation to make a difference for good in the world. The Freemasons of North America contribute substantially to charitable causes. The Shrine Masons (Shriners) operate the largest network of hospitals for burned and orthopedically impaired children in the country. The Scottish Rite Masons maintain a nationwide network of over 150 childhood language disorder clinics. The organization's publications include brochures such as *A Response to Critics of Freemasonry, Facts About Freemasonry, Get A Life: Thoughts on Freemasonry and Religion,* and *There Is No Sin in Symbols.*

OilEmpire.us
e-mail: mark@oilempire.us
Web site: www.oilempire.us

OilEmpire.us argues that the United States engineered the September 11, 2001, attacks in order to justify the seizure of oil supplies in countries such as Iraq. The group supports honest elections in the United States, practical solutions to what it considers the crisis of declining petroleum reserves, and independent media sources that expose the politics of what the organization considers the entrenched corruption of the military-industrial complex. The group's Web site offers many reports, including *Permaculture, Peak Oil and 9/11: Understanding 9/11 Paradigms; The Truth and Lies of 9/11: Good and Bad Evidence for Complicity;* and *9/11 Evidence: Official Story, Limited Hang Out, Best Evidence, Distraction Disinformation.*

Peaceful Tomorrows
PO Box 1818, Peter Stuyvesant Station
  New York, NY 10009
e-mail: membership@peacefultomorrows.org
Web site: www.peacefultomorrows.org

Peaceful Tomorrows is an organization founded by family members of those killed in the terrorist attacks of September 11, 2001, who have united to turn their grief into action for peace. By developing and advocating nonviolent options and actions in the pursuit of justice, they hope to break the cycles of violence engendered by war and terrorism. One goal of the group is to encourage a multilateral, collaborative effort to bring those responsible for the September 11 attacks to justice in accordance with the principles of international law. The group publishes newsletters that are available through its Web site.

Pentagon
Directorate for Public Inquiry and Analysis
    Washington, DC 20301-1400
(703) 545-6700
e-mail: media@defenselink.mil
Web site: www.pentagon.gov

The Pentagon is headquarters of the U.S. Department of Defense (DOD). The organization consists of approximately twenty-six thousand military and civilian employees and about three thousand nondefense support personnel dedicated to protecting the national interests of the United States. Its publications include DOD newsletters, available through its Web site. The Pentagon's Web site also offers a virtual tour of the September 11 memorial on the former site of the World Trade Center in New York.

ReOpen911.org
PO Box 3871, Santa Barbara, CA 93130
(888) 468-3784 • fax: (805) 456-0177
e-mail: http://reopen911.org/contact_us.htm
Web site: http://reopen911.org

ReOpen911.org is dedicated to opening a new investigation into the tragic attacks on September 11, 2001. The organization believes that the U.S. government is not telling the public the whole truth about the attacks. The group's intention is to bring awareness to new available evidence and to create a grassroots movement that seeks the truth of 9/11. ReOpen911.org publishes books, including *The New Pearl Harbor: Disturbing Questions About the Bush Administration and 9/11* and *The 9/11 Commission Report: Omissions And Distortions.*

Rick A. Ross Institute (RRI)

Newport Financial Center, 113 Pavonia Ave.
   #323, Jersey City, NJ 07310-1756
(201) 434-9234 • fax: (201) 435-7108
e-mail: info@rickross.com
Web site: www.rickross.com

The Rick A. Ross Institute of New Jersey is a nonprofit organization devoted to public education and research concerning cults, controversial groups, and conspiracy movements. The organization's Web site provides archives of thousands of articles, court documents, and essays about cults and conspiracies. The RRI blog also reviews and reports stories about these groups and conspiracy theories.

Bibliography

Books

Michael Barkun   *A Culture of Conspiracy: Apocalyptic Visions in Contemporary America.* Berkeley: University of California Press, 2003.

Richard Belzer   *UFOs, JFK, and Elvis: Conspiracies You Don't Have to Be Crazy to Believe.* New York: Ballantine, 1999.

David Brock   *Blinded by the Right: The Conscience of an Ex-Conservative.* New York: Crown, 2002.

Charles A. Crenshaw   *Trauma Room One: The JFK Medical Coverup Exposed.* New York: Paraview, 2001.

Mick Farren   *Conspiracies, Lies, and Hidden Agendas.* Los Angeles: Renaissance, 1999.

Robert Alan Goldberg   *Enemies Within: The Culture of Conspiracy in Modern America.* New Haven, CT: Yale University Press, 2001.

David Icke   *Alice in Wonderland and the World Trade Center Disaster: Why the Official Story of 9/11 Is a Monumental Lie.* Wildwood, MO: Bridge of Love, 2002.

Devon Jackson   *Conspiranoia! The Mother of All Conspiracy Theories.* New York: Plume, 1999.

Jim Marrs	*Inside Job: Unmasking the 9/11 Conspiracies.* San Rafael, CA: Origin, 2004.
Jim Marrs	*Rule by Secrecy: The Hidden History That Connects the Trilateral Commission, the Freemasons, and the Great Pyramids.* New York: HarperCollins, 2000.
Barr McClellan	*Blood, Money & Power: How LBJ Killed JFK.* New York: Hannover House, 2003.
Alfred W. McCoy	*The Politics of Heroin: CIA Complicity in the Global Drug Trade, Afghanistan, Southeast Asia, Central America, Colombia.* Chicago: Lawrence Hill, 2003.
Philip H. Melanson	*The Martin Luther King Assassination: New Revelations on the Conspiracy and Cover-Up, 1968–1991.* New York: Shapolsky, 1991.
William Pepper	*An Act of State: The Execution of Martin Luther King.* New York: Verso, 2003.
Daniel Pipes	*Conspiracy: How the Paranoid Style Flourishes and Where It Comes From.* New York: Free Press, 1997.
Daniel Pipes	*The Hidden Hand: Middle East Fears of Conspiracy.* New York: St. Martin's Griffin, 1998.
Kevin D. Randle	*Conspiracy of Silence.* New York: Avon, 1997.

Craig Roberts — *The Medusa File: Secret Crimes and Coverups of the U.S. Government.* Tulsa, OK: Consolidated Press International, 1997.

Gus Russo — *Live by the Sword: The Secret War Against Castro and the Death of JFK.* Baltimore: Bancroft, 1998.

Peter Dale Scott — *Drugs, Oil, and War: The United States in Afghanistan, Colombia, and Indochina.* Lanham, MD: Rowman & Littlefield, 2003.

Jonathan Vankin — *The 60 Greatest Conspiracies of All Time: History's Biggest Mysteries, Coverups, and Cabals.* New York: Barnes & Noble, 1998.

Harold Weisberg — *Oswald in New Orleans: Case of Conspiracy with the C.I.A.* New York: Canyon, 1967.

Robert Anton Wilson — *Everything Is Under Control: Conspiracies, Cults, and Cover-Ups.* New York: Quill, 1998.

David R. Wrone — *The Zapruder Film: Reframing JFK's Assassination.* Lawrence: University Press of Kansas, 2003.

Periodicals

Stephen Bates — "Haunting Diana: A British Coroner Asks Police to Investigate the Death of the Princess of Wales, Reviving All Those Wild Conspiracy Theories," *Time International,* January 19, 2004.

Dennis Behreandt   "The Rumor Mill: Conspiracies Are Real. But for Every Real Conspiracy There Are Many Unsubstantiated Rumors and Conspiracy Theories," *New American,* May 2, 2005.

Chip Berlet   "ZOG Ate My Brains: Conspiracy Theories About Jews Abound," *New Internationalist,* October 2004.

Osei Boateng   "The Poison Designed to Produce an African Disease," *New African,* November 2000.

Herb Boyd   "The Man and the Plan: Conspiracy Theories and Paranoia in Our Culture," *Black Issues Book Review,* March/April 2002.

Austin Bunn   "Conspiracy Theories: Secrecy and Power in American Culture," *Village Voice,* April 13, 1999.

Alexander Cockburn   "Forbidden Truth?" *Nation,* January 28, 2002.

Andrew Cook   "Lone Assassins: Forty Years After the Fatal Assassination of JFK," *History Today,* November 2003.

John Elvin   "George W. Bush and the Illuminati Conspiracy," *Insight on the News,* November 22, 1999.

Johann Hari   "Conspiracy Theories: A Guide." *New Statesman,* December 16, 2002.

William F. Jasper   "9-11 Conspiracy Fact & Fiction: An Abundance of Sensational and Irrational Conjecture About the September 11 Terrorist Attacks Is Being Used to Discredit Any Consideration of Conspiracy in General," *New American,* May 2, 2005.

Scott Macleod   "Suspicious Minds: In the Arab World, Conspiracy Theories and Rising Anti-Semitism Deflect Attention from Real Problems," *Time International,* June 17, 2002.

Joe Madison   "The CIA Drug Connection: Why All the Secrecy?" *Afro-American Red Star,* October 19, 1996.

Shane Miller   "Conspiracy Theories: Public Arguments as Coded Social Critiques: A Rhetorical Analysis of the TWA Flight 800 Conspiracy Theories," *Argumentation and Advocacy,* Summer 2002.

Phil Mole   "Blame It on the Jews: Anti-Semitism and the History of Jewish Conspiracy Theories," *Skeptic,* Fall 2003.

Carol Morello   "Conspiracy Theories Flourish on the Internet," *Washington Post,* October 7, 2004.

Jefferson Morley   "The Good Spy: How the Quashing of an Honest C.I.A. Investigator Helped Launch 40 Years of JFK Conspiracy Theories and Cynicism About the Feds," *Washington Monthly,* December 2003.

Sanford Robinson   "Finding Evil Within: A 'Rich Com-
                      post of Conspiracy Theories' Fuels-
                      Militias," *Jewish News of Greater
                      Phoenix,* May 17, 1996.

Samuel Sarpong   "Absurd and Blatant Lies," *World
                      Press Review,* April 1997.

Robert Sheaffer   "Where the UFO Conspiracy Theo-
                      ries Roam," *Skeptical Inquirer,* July/
                      August 2005.

Andy Smetanka   "The Truth Is WAY Out There: Crop
                      Circles, Chemtrails, UFOs, Weather
                      Control: A Beginner's Guide to the
                      Weird and Wondrous World of Mon-
                      tana Conspiracy Theories," *Missoula
                      Independent,* August 2, 2001.

Harvey   "It's a Conspiracy! The Rumor Mill
Wasserman   Grinds Out 9-11 Tales, Some Nutty
                      and Some with a Grain of Truth,"
                      Columbus Alive, July 11, 2002.

Howard Witt   "Conspiracy Theories Abound as
                      Nichols' Oklahoma Trial Begins,"
                      Knight Ridder/Tribune News Service,
                      February 29, 2004.

Index

Moby Dick Project, The (Peebles), 77
Montagnier, Luc, 33
Muslims, 21–22
mycoplasma penetrans, 33

National Cancer Institute (NCI), 34
National Commission on Terrorist Attacks upon the United States, 11
NBC, 54
Netanyahu, Benjamin, 18
New Mexico, 81–82
New Orleans Civil Air Patrol, 50
New York Times (newspaper), 53–54
Nine "9/11: Pentagon Strike" (video), 8–9
Nixon, Richard, 35
nuclear test ban treaty, 45

Office of Homeland Security, 24
Oregon State University, 39–40
Oswald, Lee Harvey, 7, 48, 50–51, 59

Pataki, George, 26
Patriot Act, 12
Peebles, Curtis, 77
Polidoro, Massimo, 57
Prados, John, 46
primates, 31, 36
Program Ash Cash, 80
Program Sky Dipper, 80
Project Apollo, 79
Project Aquarius, 76
Project Blue Book, 75
Project Gopher, 76
Project Grap Bag, 79–80
Project Horizon, 78–79
Project Moby Dick, 75, 76

Project Mogul, 72–73, 74, 83
Project Sign, 75

al Qaeda, 20

RAND study, 39–40
Rather, Dan, 56
Ray, Ellen, 52
Ray, James Earl, 41
RCA, 54
Reemtsma, Keith, 34
Ridge, Tom, 24
Roselli, Johnny, 45
Rosin, Carol, 67
Roswell mystery, 83
Ruby, Jack, 48, 55, 59, 61, 62
Russell, Richard, 49

Sarnoff, David, 54
Schiff, Steve, 83
Schiro, Victor, 47
September 11 terrorist attacks, 8, 20, 65–66
America will prevail after, 26–27
government lies about, 12–13
investigation of, 10–11
Israeli involvement in, 17–18
suspicions about, 11–12
suspicious investments prior to, 16–17
was an inside job, 13–15
see also war on terrorism
Shaw, Clay, 51, 52–53, 54, 56
Shaw, J. Gary, 55–56
Sheridan, Walter, 54
simian AIDS outbreak, 31
Skyhook program
characteristics and secrecy of, 72–73
government coverups and, 74–76